Frontispiece Leonhard Euler (1705–1783)

Leonhard Euler was born in Basle in 1707 and died in Petrograd at the age of 76 in 1783. His father was the son of a Lutheran minister who settled in Basle and the young Euler had the benefit of close friendship with the two Bernoulli brothers, Daniel and Nicholas, who both became professors of mathematics in Petrograd. Euler followed them to Russia in 1725. He lost the sight of one eye in 1735, aged only 28, and became totally blind within two or three more years. He taught himself to write formulae on a blackboard and his sons copied what he wrote, or took down equations by dictation. He was married twice and had thirteen children, of whom five survived their infancy. In spite of his blindness, and although his house was burnt to the ground in 1771 with the loss of many if not most of his papers, he was one of the most prolific authors of new mathematics of all time, covering, in particular, a wide field of mathematical analysis, the calculus and number theory. He integrated Liebnitz's differential calculus and Newton's method of fluxions into mathematical analysis. We owe to him the notations e for the base of natural logarithms and i for the square root of -1. He studied mechanics, lunar theory, elasticity, acoustics, the wave theory of light, and hydraulics. Of his completed works of nearly 900 books and papers, over half were produced after he had become completely blind. The elegance of many of his proofs have inspired generations of young mathematicians for the past two hundred years (Ball, 1908).

Most-perfect pandiagonal magic squares:

their construction and enumeration

Kathleen Ollerenshaw

and

David S. Brée

The Institute of Mathematics and its Applications

Published by the Institute of Mathematics and its Applications, Catherine Richards House, 16 Nelson Street, Southend-on-Sea, Essex SS1 1EF

Patent applied for

First published 1998

A CIP catalogue record for this book is available from the British Library

ISBN 0 905091 06 X

'Binary pair' logo by Paul Doherty and Robert Parkinson

Typeset in Great Britain by Perfect Page Publishing Services, London SW19 2RN, with TechWriter Professional by Icon Technology on an Acorn Risc PC

Printed in Great Britain by the University Press, Cambridge

Contents

Foreword   ix
Preface   xi

1 Pandiagonal magic squares   **1**
  1.1 Introduction   1
  1.2 Brief history of magic squares   3
  1.3 Pandiagonal magic squares   6
    1.3.1 Using pandiagonal Latin squares as auxiliary squares   6
    1.3.2 Paths   6
    1.3.3 There are no singly-even pandiagonal magic squares   7
    1.3.4 Mixed auxiliary squares with chess knight's paths   8
    1.3.5 A construction using primitive squares   10
  1.4 Most-perfect squares   12
  1.5 In search of a method for constructing most-perfect squares   14
  1.6 Overview   16

2 Most-perfect and reversible squares   **19**
  2.1 The need for a simpler square   19
  2.2 Most-perfect squares   20
    2.2.1 Defining most-perfect squares   20
    2.2.2 Most-perfect squares are pandiagonal magic squares   21
    2.2.3 Additional characteristic of most-perfect squares   22
  2.3 Reversible squares   23
    2.3.1 Similarity and reverse similarity   23
    2.3.2 Defining reversible squares   24
    2.3.3 Characteristics of reversible squares   25
  2.4 Transformations of reversible squares that lead to other
      reversible squares   25
    2.4.1 Legitimate transformations   26
    2.4.2 Sets of reversible squares   27
    2.4.3 A set of essentially different squares with $n = 4$ 28

2.5 Principal reversible squares   29
   2.5.1 Integers in rows/columns in ascending order and top row
              starts with 0 1   29
   2.5.2 An illustration   29
2.6 Summary   30

3 Mapping between most-perfect and doubly-even reversible squares   33
3.1 Transforming a doubly-even reversible square into a
        most-perfect square   33
   3.1.1 The transformation   33
   3.1.2 The transformation leads to a unique most-perfect square   35
3.2 Every most-perfect square can be reached from a reversible
        square   36
   3.2.1 The inverse transformation   36
   3.2.2 The inverse transformation leads to a unique reversible
              square   37
3.3 Summary   38

4 The construction of principal reversible squares   39
4.1 Principal reversible squares can be constructed from blocks   39
   4.1.1 Preliminaries   39
   4.1.2 Blocks $B(n_v, f_v)$ 40
   4.1.3 Blocks, $B_g(n_v, f_v)$, similar to the corner block $B_0(n_v, f_v)$ 40
   4.1.4 The top row determines the entire square   41
4.2 A principal reversible square must be constructed from similar
        blocks   41
   4.2.1 Gaps > 1 (if any)   42
   4.2.2 The first gap > 1 in the top row ensures that there is a
              smallest corner block   42
   4.2.3 The top n_1 rows must be filled with similar blocks   43
   4.2.4 The leftmost f_1 columns must be filled with similar blocks   44
   4.2.5 The entire square must be filled with similar blocks   45
4.3 The smallest corner block, $B_0(n_1, f_1)$ 45
4.4 Constructing successively larger corner blocks from smaller
        blocks   46
   4.4.1 Blocks similar to $B_0(n_1, f_1)$ 46
   4.4.2 Placing blocks similar to $B_0(n_1, f_1)$ along the top of the
              square   47
   4.4.3 Creating layers of blocks similar to $B_0(n_1, f_1)$ to form a
              new larger corner block $B_0(n_2, f_2)$ 47
   4.4.4 The largest corner block   48
   4.4.5 An illustration   49

4.5 Completing the square   50
4.6 The square is a principal reversible square   51

5 Enumerating the different configurations of largest corner blocks **53**
5.1 The objective   53
   5.1.1 General statement   53
   5.1.2 Strategy   54
5.2 The number of ways of choosing v progressive factors of f and
     of n 55
   5.2.1 Progressive paths through the table of factors of f 55
   5.2.2 Steps that select a progressive path 58
   5.2.3 The number of ways, $W_v(f)$, of choosing v factors from
       within the progressive paths of the f-factor table   58
   5.2.4 The value of $W_v(n)$ 59
5.3 Enumerating the different configurations $F_n(f)$ for $B_0(n, f)$ 62
5.4 Summary   62

6 Enumerating reversible squares when $n = 2^r p^s$ **63**
6.1 Ways of selecting the largest corner block   63
6.2 Summing over progressive factors   64
6.3 Rearranging binomial coefficients   65
6.4 Finding the closed form for the summation over j 66
6.5 Recombining binomial coefficients   68
6.6 Enumeration for powers of 2   70
6.7 The total number of reversible squares   71

7 Enumerating all doubly-even reversible squares   **73**
7.1 Enumerating principal reversible squares when n is doubly-even   73
7.2 The number of ways of choosing progressive factors   74
   7.2.1 One factor   75
   7.2.2 Two progressive factors   76
   7.2.3 Three progressive factors   77
   7.2.4 Any number of progressive factors   80
7.3 Enumeration for small values of n 83
7.4 Summary   84

8 Conclusion   **85**
8.1 On methods of construction   85
8.2 Construction by using Latin auxiliary squares   86
8.3 Construction by using paths   86
8.4 Construction by using the chess knight's path and mixed
     auxiliary squares   86

8.5 In conclusion   87
8.6 Summary   87

A personal perspective   **89**

Glossary   **91**
Indices and variables   91
Labels   92
Functions   93
Definition of terms   93

Appendices   **99**
A Properties of binomial coefficients   99
  A.1 Definitions   99
  A.2 A list of binomial coefficient identities   100
  A.3 The Pascal triangle   104
B Proofs of some properties of most-perfect and reversible squares   105
  B.1 Introduction   105
  B.2 Additional characteristics of most-perfect squares   105
  B.3 The sum of any pair of integers reflected in the mid-point
      of a reversible square is S 108
  B.4 Proofs of the legitimate transformations   109
  B.5 Another feature of most-perfect squares   114
C Methods for constructing pandiagonal squares   115
  C.1 Frost's method of paths   116
  C.2 Bellew's method of mixed auxiliary squares   119
  C.3 Rosser and Walker's primitive squares method   123
  C.4 McClintock's figure-of-eight method for most-perfect
       squares   128
D Construction of most-perfect squares from reversible squares   133
E Complete list of principal reversible squares of order 12   135
  E.1 No progressive factors   136
  E.2 One progressive factor   137
  E.3 Two progressive factors   144

References   147
Index   149
Do-it-yourself kit for constructing largest corner blocks   152

Foreword

by Sir Hermann Bondi, KCB, FRS, FRAS

It is a pleasure for me to write the foreword to this remarkable volume and to recommend it to the reader. The book is singular in a number of respects and should be appreciated not only directly for its contents, but over and above this for what it represents. Not only does it solve a particular, new and fascinating mathematical problem, but it does so by using new methods (developed to meet the needs of clarity) that are accessible to everybody. Whereas so much of mathematics, because of its sequential nature, requires a great deal of previous knowledge, this work starts from common understanding. Yet it has the essential characteristics of any mathematical treatise: sustained and consequential mathematical argument. Again, while so often in mathematics it needs a trained mathematical mind to understand even what the question is (let alone the solution), magic squares have intrigued mankind for centuries and their extraordinary properties contain great appeal for the untutored. Indeed the authors have selected for their treatment a particular class of magic squares, the so-called 'most-perfect squares', whose symmetry properties are so demanding that one first wonders whether there can be any examples. As this volume shows, there are in fact plenty! That the innovatory methods lead to interim results of remarkable mathematical beauty seems to be inherent in the 'magic' properties of the squares themsmelves.

It is the sustained logic, the building up of an argument step-by-step that is the mark of a truly mathematical exposition. The reader will find this characteristic beautifully displayed here. But whereas in many presentations the treatment is so abstract that one despairs of getting back to the real world, the authors are kind to the reader. Examples of real live magic squares with their manifold properties (or, rather, of the simpler 'reversible squares' that the authors prove to be their equivalent) are there on many pages so that one never gets lost in the abstract nature of the arguments.

Yet while the origin of this work lies in the readily enjoyable squares, the subject itself belongs to the deep branch of mathematics known as combin-atorics. Thus a serious and recondite topic is approached in a very appealing manner.

The first author, as a former President of the Institute of Mathematics and its Applications, is a friend of long standing who has had a most distinguished career outside mathematics. I have had the privilege to watch from afar how fascinating, enjoyable and challenging she found this undertaking. The co-author is a distinguished academic whose growing involvement with the topic it has been a pleasure to observe. Thanks to this book the reader can share in the fascination and enjoyment, while avoiding most of the effort involved in their derivation of the final result.

HERMANN BONDI

Preface

This book is dedicated to the late G.H. Hardy (1877–1947). In 1931, when I went up to Oxford as an undergraduate, Hardy was my idol, together with the great mathematician Leonhard Euler (1707–1783), the elegance of whose proofs of certain classical problems enthralled me. It was from Hardy, through my revered tutor Theodore Chaundy (1889–1966), that I first learnt to appreciate rigour and clarity in the writing of mathematics. Hardy once sent me a postcard from Trinity College, Cambridge, dated Christmas Day 1944. It was an acceptance of my first-ever submitted research paper – on critical lattices – which appeared in the *Proceedings of the Cambridge Philosophical Society*.

In his classic *Mathematician's Apology*, Hardy (1940) wrote, 'Beauty is the first test: there is no permanent place in the world for ugly mathematics'. This book is the product of an initial struggle of more than four years to provide rigorous proof of a mathematical result that I had found several years earlier and that I consider contains real beauty. An equally beautiful proof was tantalizingly elusive, teasing and challenging to the very last – but nothing less would do. I like to think that Hardy would have approved.

Interest in the problem dealt with here began with a request in 1984 from a member of the Department of Electrical Engineering at the University of Bremen, Dr Ph. W. Besslich, who had realized that pandiagonal magic squares of order $n = 8$ had useful applications in photo reproduction and image processing. He sought ways of enumerating them and of creating squares with the same properties for $n = 16$ and higher orders. He died in 1991.

The enumeration of all 'most-perfect' squares of order $n = 2^r$ ($r > 1$) that are pandiagonal magic squares with additional special properties and are defined in Chapter 1, was conjectured by me in 1987 and stated in the 25th Anniversary *IMA Bulletin* of March 1989 (Ollerenshaw, 1989). Formal publication of the proof was delayed because extensions of this result for other multiples of 4 were in sight. The full enumeration for $n = 2^r p^s$ (p any prime > 2, $r > 1$, $s \geq 0$) that forms the first part of this book was arrived at in 1989 and its existence mentioned in the *IMA Bulletin* article referred to above. However, the crux of the enumeration (and construction) that is contained in Chapter 4 and on which the result for all most-perfect squares depends had been based merely on intuition and a strict adherence to symmetries and pattern: there had been no attempt to find a rigorous proof. When a serious effort was made to provide proof, the argument became increasingly complex and involved numerous diversions that had their own interest. The full proof thus became unsuitable for publication as an article in a recognized journal and better suited to publication as a book. From the beginning of the search for proof, I have always had the comfort and certainty of an assuredly correct answer. The algebraic 'discoveries' emerging during the course of the work – new to me if not to others – have been a continuing source of elation.

My inclination in trying to solve problems of this kind is to follow patterns of behaviour and work from the particular to the general – no basis whatever for dealing with functions that are to extend to infinity, particularly when, as here, the resulting equations are not amenable to the classic method of proof by induction. Instead, the proof of the construction and initial formulae for the enumeration of squares has been arrived at through logical argument. At every stage, the central issue has been that of binomial coefficients, typically 'in how many different ways can these particular choices be made from those several possibilities?'. The final formula for the enumeration itself has been deduced, in Chapter 6, by applying the appropriate algebraic identities involving series of binomial coefficients found (usually in different format from my own) in the textbook *Concrete Mathematics* (Graham, Knuth and Patashnik, 1989).

In the preliminary stages, when I first began to put the ideas onto paper, I was greatly helped by Ronald Flude, who had recently retired from the research and teaching staff of the Department of Computer Studies at the University of Lancaster. I started off on many false trails. It was his criticisms that forced me to bring back into line the wilder ideas, and helped me to lay sound foundations for the early chapters. My gratitude for his advice at the beginning and for his continued interest is profound.

I am particularly indebted to Sir Hermann Bondi for his interest, encouragement and advice throughout a rather lengthy development from our joint paper of 1982 on magic squares of order $n = 4$ (Ollerenshaw and Bondi, 1982), and my subsequent enumeration of most-perfect squares of order $n = 8$ (Ollerenshaw, 1986), to this present proof for all most-perfect squares.

I owe much to my schools and university: Ladybarn House School, then in Manchester, a Montessori school with a brilliant ex-Girton headmistress; St Leonards School, St Andrews, of which I am privileged to be president; and Somerville College, Oxford, where I gained a scholarship in mathematics in 1931 and was made an Honorary Fellow in 1977. My thanks go to many others for the patience and tolerance they have afforded me during my obsessive concentration on bringing this book to a satisfactory finish. Special thanks go to Dr M.B. Goatly of Perfect Page Publishing Services. His extensive experience of editorship with the Royal Society; his expertise, professional skill and instinctive understanding of what has been required in laying out equations, tables and text in camera-ready form, and his meticulous accuracy have been the greatest possible comfort both in anticipation and in execution. Staff of the John Rylands University Library of Manchester have been notably helpful from the beginning in searching the incomparably fine collections of mathematical publications of the past 300 years. The Greater Manchester County Headquarters of St John Ambulance have provided me with frequent access to their facilities over several years. Special thanks go to the late Paul Doherty, the distinguished British astrocartographer. His colour drawing forms the base of the cover design. It depicts a pair of binary stars in the red giant α-Hercules, the matter from the smaller star pouring into the larger star. Paul died of cancer, aged 50, on 26 November 1997, perhaps his last of many kindnesses being that he sent his slide with a covering note wishing the book success. I am grateful to Robert Parkinson of the Manchester Astronomical Society for adapting Paul's drawing, and to the Institute of Mathematics and its Applications for stalwart support from the beginning in the writing of this book.

KATHLEEN OLLERENSHAW

My interest in magic squares stems from a research seminar at which my supervisor, Professor Herbert A. Simon, used the equivalence between the games of number scrabble and noughts and crosses (tic-tac-toe) via the 3 by 3 magic square, to demonstrate the power of good representations, a lesson that I have never forgotten. But for my interest and any small ability in mathematics, I wish to thank two of my teachers at The King's School, Canterbury, Mr Paul Pollock and Mr Richard Painter. To find, many years later, that my neighbour had developed a method for constructing and enumerating most-perfect squares of 'any' size, was so fascinating that I offered to proof read her manuscript over Easter 1995. It took me two years to appreciate fully what she had intrinsically grasped long before. Finally my thanks go to the Computer Science Department of Manchester University for freeing me from obligations so that I could work on this book, and to Stanford University for being so conducive to research.

DAVID BRÉE

1
Pandiagonal magic squares

1.1 Introduction

Magic squares have had wide popular appeal among mathematicians over many centuries, interest in them waxing and waning according to contemporary activity in scientific and mathematical thought. Magic squares of a particular kind, called 'pandiagonal', have a property that makes them of special interest. Magic squares were known as early as A.D. 1300 and probably long before that. At the turn of this present century interest largely centred on squares for which n (where n^2 is the number of integers forming the square) is an odd number; squares for even values of n (other than $n = 4$) appeared to be not only of less interest, but considerably more difficult to find.

In general, magic squares, and particularly pandiagonal magic squares, are not easy to construct. Except for special values of n, it is extremely hard to count how many there are as this first requires a method of construction that will generate **all** squares of a given size. Enumeration is interesting in its own right, and can also be critical for some applications.

Renewed interest in magic, and pandiagonal, squares over the past decade has been stimulated partly by the prospect of potential applications in advanced computer programming and image processing. The precision essential to methods leading to computer programming has necessitated a more rigorous proof of the underlying mathematics than was probably considered necessary a hundred years ago. This makes acceptable proofs of results harder to follow and, usually, of greater length than they used to be – returning full circle to the absolute rigour demanded by philosophers in ancient Greece, particularly when the elusive idea of infinity is involved.

The modern combinatorial (as opposed to recreational) method of creating magic squares has been based on simpler Latin squares (Euler, 1779; Dénes and Keedwell, 1974; Brouwer, 1991). This has had significant success, but does not purport to give all magic squares for any particular order n, and so does not lead to a method of enumeration. Until now, as far as the authors are aware, no complete enumeration has been given for all pandiagonal squares.

More recently, Ollerenshaw developed an entirely different approach to the creation of a class of pandiagonal squares of doubly-even order n (the value of n must be a multiple of 4). These squares are given the name 'most-perfect', a description first used by McClintock (1897) in which a method of constructing this class of the pandiagonal squares of even order was presented. A novel method of construction of all possible most-perfect squares is given here, based on a transformation from squares named 'reversible'. This provides a direct method of constructing all most-perfect squares (but not all pandiagonal magic squares, which was the original objective) for values of n that can extend to infinity. More significantly, a formula giving the number of **all** most-perfect squares for **any** value of n has been established.

Even for small values of n, the gross totals are astronomical in size. For example, when $n = 36$ there are 2.7×10^{44} essentially different most-perfect squares, a number so great that the chance of the fastest teraflop computer in the world finding a particular most-perfect square by trial and error in 20 billion years (an upper bound of the age of the universe) is less than one in a billion billion.* To understand how this has been done, we begin with some definitions.

A MAGIC SQUARE consists of different integers arranged in the form of a square so that the sum of these integers in every row, in every column and in each of the two principal diagonal is the same. Any magic square can be subjected to a reflection in its central horizontal and/or vertical axes and/or a reflection in a principal diagonal without losing its magic character. Squares are said to be ESSENTIALLY DIFFERENT if they cannot be transformed into one another by any combination of these reflections. If elements forming a magic square are the n^2 consecutive positive integers 1 to n^2 inclusive, or, alternatively, the integers 0 to $(n^2 - 1)$, the square is said to be NORMAL and of the nth order. The sum of the integers on every row, column and in the two principal diagonals is then, clearly, $\frac{1}{2}n(n^2 + 1)$ or $\frac{1}{2}n(n^2 - 1)$, respectively.

If the rows and columns of a magic square of order n are repeated indefinitely to form an extended array, as illustrated below with $n = 4$, then any n integers read in sequence along an extended diagonal line of the array forms a BROKEN DIAGONAL of the original square. A magic square in which

---

* The age of the universe is estimated at between 10 and 20 billion (10^9) years (David Black, `http//cass.jsc.nasa.gov/newsletters/lpib/lpib77/black77.html`). There are 32 million seconds a year. A teraflop machine performs 10^{12} floating-point operations a second. Assuming that the machine can check one square per floating-point operation, it could have checked 6.4×10^{28} squares since the Big Bang. So the chances of finding a particular square from among the 2.7×10^{44} other squares is one in 3.5×10^{15}.

all diagonals, that is the broken diagonals as well as the principal diagonals, add to the same sum is described as PANDIAGONAL.

Pandiagonal squares of order n have the property that, when the rows and columns are repeated indefinitely without rotation, that is either horizontally or vertically, to form a new larger array of width and depth both $\geq 2n$, then any square of order n within this array is also pandiagonal magic. As illustration, consider the pandiagonal magic square of order 4 shown in Figure 1.1.1, and extend it in the manner described above to give the array in Figure 1.1.2. Then the square with integers printed in bold with 2 in its top left corner is also pandiagonal magic.

```
 0  11   6  13
14   5   8   3
 9   2  15   4
 7  12   1  10
```

Figure 1.1.1 A 4 by 4 pandiagonal square.

```
 0  11   6  13   0  11   6  13
14   5   8   3  14   5   8   3
 9   2  15   4   9   2  15   4
 7  12   1  10   7  12   1  10
 0  11   6  13   0  11   6  13
14   5   8   3  14   5   8   3
 9   2  15   4   9   2  15   4
 7  12   1  10   7  12   1  10
```

Figure 1.1.2 A 4 by 4 pandiagonal square embedded in an array.

1.2 Brief history of magic squares

Magic squares have a long history (Andrews, 1917; Kraitchik, 1930; Ball, 1939). The (unique) 3 by 3 magic square using the numbers 1 to 9, namely

```
2  9  4
7  5  3
6  1  8,
```

which is known as the *lo-shu*, is said to have been brought to man by a turtle from the river Lo in the days of the legendary Emperor Yii of China *circa* 2000 BC, but most probably dates from around 1000 AD. Martin Gardner (1996) has on offer a prize for anyone who can devise a 3 by 3 non-normal magic square consisting of nine square numbers. In pursuing this problem, Lee Sallows (1997) has recently discovered a remarkable relationship between 3 by 3 magic squares involving complex numbers and 'off-centre' parallelograms.

Albrecht Dürer's famous picture '*Melencolia I*', hung in the British Museum, shows the 4 by 4 (symmetrical) magic square given in Figure 1.2.1, in which the date of the picture, 1514, appears in the two middle cells of the

$$
\begin{array}{cccc}
16 & 3 & 2 & 13 \\
5 & 10 & 11 & 8 \\
9 & 6 & 7 & 12 \\
4 & 15 & 14 & 1
\end{array}
$$

Figure 1.2.1 Dürer's 4 by 4 symmetrical magic square.

bottom row. The integers in the rows, columns, principal diagonals and the two 'short' broken diagonals, namely

$$
\begin{array}{cccc}
5 & 3 & 14 & 12, \\
2 & 8 & 9 & 15,
\end{array}
$$

add respectively to 34, and integers that are reflections in the centre are complements adding to $\frac{1}{2} \times 34 = 17$. A brief account of the history of the 4 by 4 magic square is given in the introduction to the paper 'Magic squares of order four' by Ollerenshaw and Bondi (1982), who gave the first analytical proof that Bernard Frénicle de Bessey's (1693) listing of 880 4 by 4 magic squares was complete.

Over the centuries a great deal of work has been done on the construction of magic squares of odd order. Benjamin Franklin (1706–1790) confessed to spending untold hours developing magic squares of increasingly large odd order, before putting this firmly aside and becoming a politician and diplomat of the greatest distinction.

One method of constructing magic squares is from orthogonal AUXILIARY SQUARES A and A', with integers $a_{i,j}$ and $a'_{i,j}$ such that $0 \leq \{a_{i,j}, a'_{i,j}\} < n$ and such that each of the integers 0, 1, ..., $(n - 1)$ occurs exactly n times in each of A and A'. A will be called the RADIX AUXILIARY and A' the UNIT AUXILIARY. The two squares, A and A', are ORTHOGONAL if all ordered pairs of integers in the same position in both squares, $(a_{i,j}, a'_{i,j})$, are different. Then the square $nA + A'$ contains each of the integers 0, 1, ..., $(n^2 - 1)$ exactly once. Euler (1779), in his search for the solution to the six officers problem,[*] noted that if the auxiliary squares are Latin squares then the sum is a semi-

---

[*] The six officers problem: 36 officers are chosen, six from each of six different regiments and six from each of six different ranks. They are to be placed in six groups of six officers in such a way that in each group there is one officer from every regiment and one officer of every rank. Euler suspected that there could be no solution to this problem, but he did not succeed in proving this. A proof was found in 1890 by Tarry (Kraitchik, 1930, p. 159). Euler's search led him to develop his method for constructing semi-magic squares.

magic square, i.e. a square in which the rows and columns, but not necessarily the principal diagonals, have a constant sum.

If A and A' are a pair of orthogonal diagonal Latin squares then the square $nA + A'$ is a magic square, P. A DIAGONAL LATIN SQUARE, A, of order n, is an n by n array such that every row, every column and the two principal diagonals are a permutation of $\{0, 1, \dots , (n-1)\}$, so each row, column and principal diagonal sums to $\frac{1}{2}n(n-1)$. The integers of P, $p_{i,j}$, are then $na_{i,j} + a'_{i,j}$ and P has the properties of a magic square as:

- the row sums are

$$\sum_j p_{i,j} = n \sum_j a_{i,j} + \sum_j a'_{i,j} = \tfrac{1}{2}n^2(n-1) + \tfrac{1}{2}n(n-1) = \tfrac{1}{2}n(n^2-1);$$

- the column sums are

$$\sum_i p_{i,j} = n \sum_i a_{i,j} + \sum_i a'_{i,j} = \tfrac{1}{2}n^2(n-1) + \tfrac{1}{2}n(n-1) = \tfrac{1}{2}n(n^2-1);$$

- the sums of the principal diagonals are

$$\sum_i p_{i,i} = n \sum_i a_{i,i} + \sum_i a'_{i,i} = \tfrac{1}{2}n(n^2-1)$$

and

$$\sum_i p_{i,n-i} = n \sum_i a_{i,n-i} + \sum_i a'_{i,n-i} = \tfrac{1}{2}n(n^2-1).$$

It has recently been shown that pairs of orthogonal diagonal Latin squares exist for all values of $n \neq \{2,3,6\}$ (Brown *et al.*, 1993). It might therefore be thought that most magic squares of order $n \neq \{2,3,6\}$ could be constructed by first constructing all pairs of orthogonal Latin squares. Indeed the magic square shown in Figure 1.1.1 can be so constructed from the pair of orthogonal Latin squares shown in Figure 1.2.2. However, this is not so in general. For instance the 4 by 4 magic square shown in Figure 1.2.3 is made up of two auxiliary squares, neither of which is a Latin square. To date there has been no method, other than trial and error, of constructing **all** magic squares for any given $n > 5$.

	A					A'		
0	2	1	3		0	3	2	1
3	1	2	0		2	1	0	3
2	0	3	1		1	2	3	0
1	3	0	2		3	0	1	2

Figure 1.2.2 Auxiliary orthogonal Latin squares for the magic square in Figure 1.1.1.

Magic square	=		$4 \times A$		+		A'	
0	14	3	13		0	3	0	3		0	2	3	1
7	9	4	10		1	2	1	2		3	1	0	2
12	2	15	1		3	0	3	0		0	2	3	1
11	5	8	6		2	1	2	1		3	1	0	2

Figure 1.2.3 Another 4 by 4 magic square and its auxiliary squares.

1.3 Pandiagonal magic squares

1.3.1 Using pandiagonal Latin squares as auxiliary squares

Because of the difficulty in constructing all magic squares for large n, attention has been paid to constructing a subset of the magic squares, namely the pandiagonal magic squares in which all the diagonals, the broken as well as the principal diagonals, have a constant sum.

Euler (1779) noticed that his method of auxiliary squares could produce pandiagonal squares. His illustration of a 7 by 7 pandiagonal square is shown in Figure 1.3.1*a*; it is also shown to the base 7 in Figure 1.3.1*b* so that its pandiagonal property is clear. A sufficient condition for constructing a pandiagonal magic square by this method is that the auxiliary squares are a pair of orthogonal PANDIAGONAL LATIN SQUARES, i.e. Latin squares in which each of the diagonals, the broken as well as the principal diagonals, sums to $\frac{1}{2}n(n-1)$. For, in addition to being a magic square, all the diagonal sums are $\Sigma_i p_{i,j\pm i} = n\Sigma_i a_{i,j\pm i} + \Sigma_i a_{j\pm i,i} = \frac{1}{2}n^2(n-1) + \frac{1}{2}n(n-1) = \frac{1}{2}n(n^2-1)$. There-fore, provided that orthogonal pandiagonal Latin squares can be constructed, so can pandiagonal magic squares. It has recently been shown that a self-orthogonal pandiagonal Latin square, and hence a pandiagonal magic square, can be constructed for any order n except n modulo 4 = 2 and n modulo 9 = 3 (Xu and Lu, 1995). However, not all pandiagonal magic squares of these orders can be constructed by using this method, not even for $n = 4$, as shown by the magic square in Figure 1.2.3, which is pandiagonal but not constructed from Latin auxiliary squares.

(a)								(b)						
40	7	16	3	22	32	48		55	10	22	3	31	44	66
25	34	47	35	9	17	1		34	46	65	50	12	23	1
10	15	4	27	33	42	37		13	21	4	36	45	60	52
28	44	38	8	18	6	26		40	62	53	11	24	6	35
20	5	21	30	45	36	11		26	5	30	42	63	51	14
43	39	13	19	0	23	31		61	54	16	25	0	32	43
2	24	29	46	41	12	14		2	33	41	64	56	15	20

Figure 1.3.1 Euler's pandiagonal magic square of order 7:
(*a*) in decimal; (*b*) to the base 7.

1.3.2 Paths

Euler's discovery of pandiagonal squares went unnoticed for almost a hundred years (Kraitchik, 1930, p. 211), until, in 1866, Frost (1866, 1878)[*]

---

[*] The Revd Andrew Hollingworth Frost (1820–1907), a mathematics wrangler of St John's College, Cambridge, was a church missionary in Nasik, Bombay, from 1855 to 1867. During his absence abroad the earlier paper was presented to the *Quarterly Journal* by his younger brother, the Revd Percival Frost, also a wrangler and later a Fellow of St Johns, who called the squares 'Nasik'. Neither brother seemed aware of Euler's earlier discovery of pandiagonal squares.

published a method for constructing pandiagonal magic squares, also based on first constructing a pair of orthogonal auxiliary squares, each containing n copies of the integers 0, 1, ..., $(n - 1)$, but not necessarily of Latin design. The copies of any one integer are arranged along a path, the same path being used for all the integers within an auxiliary square. A path, starting at any position, moves at each step either one row down and c columns left or right, or r rows down and one column left or right, where $1 < \{r, c\} < (n - 1)$. The possible paths are thus $(1, \pm2)$, $(1, \pm3)$, ..., $(1, \pm(n - 2))$ and $(2, \pm1)$, $(3, \pm1)$, ..., $((n - 2), \pm1)$, where the first integer indicates the number of rows to move down and the second indicates the number of columns to move right (or left, if negative). For a path to be PERMISSIBLE, it must return to the position in which it started. (Reversing both signs gives another set of initial moves starting upward, but these are the same paths traversed in the reverse direction.) For the auxiliary squares to be orthogonal, two different paths must be selected, one for each of the two auxiliary squares; the two paths selected must intersect only in their common starting point. The integers in one of the auxiliary squares are then multiplied by n. An illustration of this process for $n = 4$ is shown in Figure 1.2.3, where the path $(2, 1)$ is used for constructing A and the path $(1, 2)$ for constructing A'. A description of Frost's method is given in Appendix C.1.

The integers in both of the auxiliary squares must be arranged along paths. For example, the auxiliary squares shown in Figure 1.2.2 cannot be constructed by this method, as the integers do not lie along paths; as a result the 4 by 4 pandiagonal square shown in Figure 1.1.1 cannot be constructed using the method of paths.

Several methods for generating pandiagonal squares have been put forward over the years, particularly around the turn of the last century, e.g. that of Margossian (Ball, 1939) which is based on Galois arithmetic. However, these methods, too, were not complete, i.e. they did not generate all pandiagonal squares of a given order.

1.3.3 There are no singly-even pandiagonal magic squares

It was proved by C. Planck (1919, pp. 308–309) that **there are no pandiagonal magic squares of singly-even order**, i.e. where n modulo 4 = 2. Planck stated that the result was well known, but, as far as he was aware, previously unproved. In this he was mistaken as it had already been proved, although less elegantly, by Frost (1878) forty years earlier! As this fact is critical to our argument, it seems expedient to give Planck's elegant proof in full here.

Consider Figure 1.3.3, representing part of the top rows and leftmost columns of a completed normal square of order n, consisting of the n^2 integers 0 to $(n^2 - 1)$. Let $k = \frac{1}{2}n$. Mark the cells forming the square as in Figure 1.3.3. For the square to be pandiagonal magic the integers in the

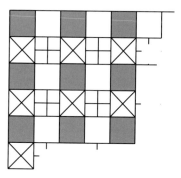

Figure 1.3.3 Illustration of the top left cells of a pandiagonal square
(after Planck (1919)).

rows, the columns and in all diagonals (the broken diagonals as well as the principal diagonals) must have the same sum, namely $\frac{1}{2}n(n^2 - 1)$ $= k(4k^2 - 1) = Z$, say.

Let the sum of the integers in all the shaded cells of the completed square be A, in all the blank cells be B, and in all the cells with St Andrew's crosses be C. Then, for the completed square to be pandiagonal magic, the sum of the integers in all the alternate rows containing shaded and blank cells is $A + B = kZ$. Likewise, the sum of the integers in all the columns containing shaded cells and cells with St Andrew's crosses is $A + C = kZ$. Also, for even n, the sum of the integers in the 'upward slanting diagonals', consisting of the blank cells and cells with St Andrew's crosses, is $B + C = kZ$. These equalities yield $A = B = C = \frac{1}{2}kZ = 2k^4 - \frac{1}{2}k^2$ $= \frac{1}{8}(n^4 - n^2)$. Therefore no such square can exist when k is odd, i.e. when n is singly-even, for then $\frac{1}{2}kZ$ would be fractional. So pandiagonal squares of even order must be doubly-even.

Planck went on to show how to construct (and enumerate) non-normal pandiagonal magic squares of orders 6 and 10, i.e. when the integers that form the square are not consecutive.

1.3.4 Mixed auxiliary squares with chess knight's paths

Recently the chess knight's path method for constructing magic squares has been adapted by Bellew (1997) to construct pandiagonal squares. The adaptation requires a preliminary step in which the auxiliary squares are constructed by placing letters along a chess KNIGHT'S PATH, i.e. one of the following paths: $(1, \pm2)$ $(2, \pm1)$. Here, to conform with Euler's method, Latin letters are used for one auxiliary square and Greek letters for the other.[*] The two knight's paths may only intersect at their common starting position, e.g.

[*] Bellew uses lower-case and capital Latin letters.

at (0,0). They are then called NON-INTERSECTING PATHS. The choice of non-intersecting knight's paths ensures that the two auxiliary squares are orthogonal. In general, for instance when n is prime, there are $4 \times 3 = 12$ possible combinations of paths. However, when n is a multiple of 2, 3 or 5 some of the knight's paths intersect at positions in addition to their common starting point and so fewer pairs of non-intersecting paths are available. When n is a multiple of $2 \times 3 \times 5 = 30$, there are no non-intersecting knight's paths.

Once a pair of auxiliary squares has been constructed using n Latin and n Greek letters, these letters are associated with integers. The letters a and α are both associated with the integer 0. The remaining $2(n-1)$ letters are associated with $2(n-1)$ unique integers taken from the range 1 to $(n-1)n$ in such a way that when the two auxiliary squares are simply added, every integer from 0 to $(n^2 - 1)$ occurs once and only once. Call a pair of auxiliary squares constructed in this manner MIXED AUXILIARY SQUARES.

For example, with $n = 4$ there are only two knight's paths, namely $(1, 2)$ and $(2, 1)$, as $(1, -2)$ and $(2, -1)$ are the same as $(1, 2)$ and $(2, 1)$ respectively. A pair of auxiliary squares is shown in Figure 1.3.4a. The requirement is for rows to have the same sum: $\alpha + \gamma = \beta + \delta$; and for columns to have the same sum: $a + c = b + d$. There are three assignments of integers to letters that satisfy this requirement, as shown in Figure 1.3.4b. For $n = 4$ there are $8 \times (4/2)! = 16$ ways of arranging these auxiliary squares, giving $3 \times 16 = 48$ essentially different 4 by 4 pandiagonal squares. A complete description of this method is given in Appendix C.2.

(*a*) Auxiliary squares:

a	b	c	d	α	γ	α	γ
c	d	a	b	β	δ	β	δ
a	b	c	d	γ	α	γ	α
c	d	a	b	δ	β	δ	β

(*b*) Three possible assignments:

a	b	c	d	α	β	γ	δ
0	1	3	2	0	4	12	8
0	1	5	4	0	2	10	8
0	1	9	8	0	2	6	4

(*c*) Three resulting pandiagonal squares:

0	13	3	14	0	11	5	14	0	7	9	14
7	10	4	9	7	12	2	9	11	12	2	5
12	1	15	2	10	1	15	4	6	1	15	8
11	6	8	5	13	6	8	3	13	10	4	3

Figure 1.3.4 Constructing 4 by 4 pandiagonal squares by mixed auxiliaries.

Bellew gives formulae for the number of arrangements for pairs of auxiliary squares; for example for n not divisible by 2, 3 or 5, the number is $12 \times (n!)^2$. But as there is no general method for assigning integers to letters, there is no general formula for the total number of pandiagonal magic squares that can be generated by this method. Moreover, there exist self-orthogonal pandiagonal Latin squares, and hence also pandiagonal magic squares, for n a multiple of $180 = 6 \times 30$ (Xu and Lu, 1995), but these squares cannot be generated by this method as there are no non-intersecting knight's paths when n is a multiple of 30.

1.3.5 A construction using primitive squares

A very different method for constructing pandiagonal magic squares begins by constructing 'primitive' squares and transforming these into pandiagonal squares (Rosser and Walker, 1939). **Primitive squares** have the property of **equal cross sums**, that is the sum of the integers at one pair of opposite corners of any rectangle in the square is the same as the sum of the integers at the other pair of opposite corners. If $q_{i,j}$ are the integers in the square Q, then Q is primitive if $q_{i,j} + q_{i',j'} = q_{i,j'} + q_{i',j}$. Rosser and Walker showed that transforming a primitive square by

$$T = \begin{bmatrix} a & c \\ b & d \end{bmatrix}, \qquad\qquad (1.3.5.1)$$

that is, the integer at (i, j) is moved to the position $(ai + cj, \; bi + dj)$, gives a pandiagonal magic square, provided that $abcd\,(a^2 - b^2)\,(c^2 - d^2)$ is prime to n.

If the rows or columns of a primitive square are permuted, it is still a primitive square and so any primitive square can be transformed into a NORMALIZED PRIMITIVE SQUARE in which the integers in the top row and the left column are in ascending order. Moreover if the integer at $(0, 1)$ is larger than that at $(1, 0)$ then the integers can be reflected in the main diagonal so that the integer at $(0, 1)$ is now less than the integer at $(1, 0)$, while still preserving equal cross sums. In the resulting normalized primitive square, $q_{i,j} \leq q_{i',j'}$ if $i \leq i'$ and $j \leq j'$. The number of primitive squares that can be transformed by these permutations into a single normalized primitive square is therefore $2\,(n!)^2$. A similar idea will be used in this book (Section 4.4.4).

The resulting magic square is made up of two auxiliary squares in which the integers are arranged in paths $(1, r)$ and $(u, 1)$, where $1 < \{r, u\} < n$, as shown in Figure 1.3.5. To reveal the two auxiliary squares from which the pandiagonal magic square is constructed, the integers are shown to base 11, with the letter A indicating 10.

When 2 is a factor of n, there are no transforms of the form (1.3.5.1) that satisfy the proviso that $abcd\,(a^2 - b^2)\,(c^2 - d^2)$ be prime to n. The reason is that then a, b, c and d would all have to be odd and consequently $(a^2 - b^2)$ and $(c^2 - d^2)$ would be even and so not prime to n. However, there are transforms of the form (1.3.5.1) that take primitive squares into pandiagonal squares. For instance the transform

$$T = \begin{bmatrix} 1 & 2 \\ 2 & 3 \end{bmatrix}$$

takes the three primitive squares of Figure 1.3.6a into the three 4 by 4 pandiagonal squares shown in Figure 1.3.4c. That these are indeed primitive squares can be seen by permuting rows and columns, an operation that leaves a primitive square primitive, to give the three normalized primitive squares shown in Figure 1.3.6c.

00	18	25	32	4A	57	64	71	89	96	A3
91	A9	06	13	20	38	45	52	6A	77	84
72	8A	97	A4	01	19	26	33	40	58	65
53	60	78	85	92	AA	07	14	21	39	46
34	41	59	66	73	80	98	A5	02	1A	27
15	22	3A	47	54	61	79	86	93	A0	08
A6	03	10	28	35	42	5A	67	74	81	99
87	94	A1	09	16	23	30	48	55	62	7A
68	75	82	9A	A7	04	11	29	36	43	50
49	56	63	70	88	95	A2	0A	17	24	31
2A	37	44	51	69	76	83	90	A8	05	12

Figure 1.3.5 An 11 by 11 pandiagonal square, with integers to base 11, with A indicating 10, showing its two auxiliary squares with paths $(1, 2)$ and $(3, 1)$.

(a) Primitive squares

```
0   2   3   1
4   6   7   5
12  14  15  13
8   10  11  9

0   4   5   1
2   6   7   3
10  14  15  11
8   12  13  9

0   8   9   1
2   10  11  3
6   14  15  7
4   12  13  5
```

(b) Permute cols 0 and 3 and shift cols one right

```
0   1   2   3
4   5   6   7
12  13  14  15
8   9   10  11

0   1   4   5
2   3   6   7
10  11  14  15
8   9   12  13

0   1   8   9
2   3   10  11
6   7   14  15
4   5   12  13
```

(c) Permute rows 2 and 3

```
0   1   2   3
4   5   6   7
8   9   10  11
12  13  14  15

0   1   4   5
2   3   6   7
8   9   12  13
10  11  14  15

0   1   8   9
2   3   10  11
4   5   12  13
6   7   14  15
```

Figure 1.3.6 Three 4 by 4 primitive squares and their normalized forms.

Rosser and Walker's method, as described in Appendix C.3, constructs all pandiagonal magic squares for $n = \{1, 4, 5\}$ (which had already been known for a long time) and some, but not necessarily all, pandiagonal squares for any other n, $n \neq 3$ and n modulo $4 \neq 2$ (for which, as was known, there are no pandiagonal squares). When n is a prime > 2, the total number of pandiagonal squares that can be constructed by this method is $(n!)^2 (n - 3) (n - 4)$. However, Rosser and Walker do not have a general formula for the enumeration when n is not prime and > 5. Moreover, as they show (in their Theorem 1.6), for any $n \neq \{1, 3, 4, 5\}$ and n modulo $4 \neq 2$ there are pandiagonal squares that cannot be constructed with the transform (1.3.5.1).

1.4 Most-perfect squares

It is more than a century since Frost (1878) published his paper on pandiagonal magic squares, and it is still not possible to enumerate them in general. This suggests that attention should be turned to a restricted subset of such squares.

In 1897 Eamon McClintock, at Toronto University, published a paper in which he defined and gave a method of construction for a particular type of pandiagonal magic square of doubly-even order n, which are here called most-perfect. In addition to being pandiagonal, MOST-PERFECT squares, for example that in Figure 1.1.1, which is most-perfect, are defined as having the properties that (i) the integers forming any small 2×2 array within the extended array formed by transpositions and/or reflections, illustrated in Figure 1.1.2, sum to $2(n^2 - 1)$; (ii) each integer is complementary to the one distant from it $\frac{1}{2}n$ places in the same diagonal. It was this paper of Eamon McClintock's and an unrelated request in 1985 from the late Dr Besslich (1983) of the Department of Electrical Engineering of Bremen University, that stimulated the investigation undertaken here.

McClintock's method requires first that MCCLINTOCK SQUARES be constructed in which:

(i) the even rows are 'similar' and the odd rows are 'similar';
(ii) for any pair of adjacent rows, all VERTICAL COUPLETS, i.e. pairs of adjacent integers in the same column, have a constant sum;
(iii) integers in the bottom half of the square are complements, with respect to $(n^2 - 1)$, of the corresponding integers, distant $\frac{1}{2}n$ along a diagonal, in the top half of the square.

An example of a McClintock square, generated by the only method he specified which is based on a figure-of-eight, is shown in Figure 1.4 with integers in octal. To transform McClintock squares into most-perfect squares, the integers in odd columns in the top half of the square are replaced by their complements with respect to $(n^2 - 1)$. The bottom half of the square is emptied and refilled with integers that are complements, with respect to $(n^2 - 1)$, of integers distant $\frac{1}{2}n$ along a diagonal in the top half of

```
 0  1  2  3 | 13 12 11 10
17 16 15 14    4  5  6  7
20 21 22 23   33 32 31 30
37 36 35 34   24 25 26 27
  ‑          +           ‑
40 41 42 43   53 52 51 50
57 56 55 54   44 45 46 47
60 61 62 62   73 72 71 70
77 76 75 74 | 64 65 66 67
```

Figure 1.4 An 8 by 8 McClintock square, in octal.

the square. McClintock established that there was a one-to-one correspondence between his squares and most-perfect squares. However, the figure-of-eight method generates only some of these squares and McClintock did not provide methods for constructing all his squares. See Appendix C.4 for details.

The number of essentially different most-perfect squares of order $n = 4$ (although not defined as such) had been known for some 300 years to be 48, namely $N_4 = 3$ multiplied by $M_4 = 2^{(4-2)}(2!)^2 = 16$. One square from each set has been given in Figure 1.3.4.

In 1986 Ollerenshaw established, using McClintock's transformation but an extended method of construction, that the most-perfect squares of order $n = 8$ could be derived from just $N_8 = 10$ squares multiplied by an expression, say M_n, where here $M_8 = 2^6(4!)^2 = 38,864$. N_n is the number of 'principal reversible' squares with 0 in the top left corner, whereas M_n takes account of transformations.

The progression $N_4 = 3$, $N_8 = 10$ when $n = 2^2$, $n = 2^3$ respectively gave a clue to results for all values of n that are powers of 2. In the usual nomenclature of combinations, where $\binom{u}{v} = u! / \{v! (u - v)!\}$ represents the number of ways of choosing v objects from u objects, the values $N_4 = 3$, $N_8 = 10$ are, respectively, the number of ways of choosing 2 objects from 3 objects, namely $\binom{3}{2}$, and the number of ways of choosing 3 objects from 5 objects, namely $\binom{5}{3}$. It will be shown in Section 6.6 that the total number of most-perfect squares of order $n = 2^r$, N_{2^r}, can be derived from just such a combination $\binom{2r-1}{r}$, which is the number of different ways of fitting the $(2r - 1)$ factors of 2^r other than 1 and 2^r itself into r positions to form essentially different squares. The expression for M_n enumerates the 'set' of possible permutations of rows and/or columns of the squares that leave the most-perfect property of the square unchanged, giving

$$M_{2^r} = 2^{(2^r - 2)}\{(2^{r-1})!\}^2.$$

This result was stated in Ollerenshaw's I.M.A. Christmas Lecture in Coventry in 1987, which appeared as an article 'Living mathematics' published in the *Bulletin of the Institute of Mathematics* in 1989, where McClintock's squares were also briefly described.

When n is not a power of 2, results become more complex. For example, the number, N_{12}, of most-perfect squares of order $n = 12$ with 0 in the top left corner from which all 12 by 12 most-perfect squares can be derived, is greater than N_{16}, the number of equivalent most-perfect squares for $n = 16$.

1.5 In search of a method for constructing most-perfect squares

Although McClintock (1897) showed that there is a one-to-one correspondence between McClintock squares and most-perfect squares, his method of construction of such squares is under-specified. An extension of this method by Ollerenshaw (1986) is not suitable for generalization. A further (unpublished) extension enabled the generation of all squares when $n = 2^r p^s$ (p any prime > 2, integers $r > 1$, $s \geq 0$), providing a conjecture for the number of most-perfect squares of this order (Ollerenshaw, 1989). This further extension concerned the behaviour of sequences of consecutive integers of lengths f_v, say, where f_v is a multiple of f_{v-1} and a factor of n. However, a proof that this method produced all McClintock squares was elusive. So another method needed to be found.

The methods for constructing pandiagonal squares outlined in Section 1.3 might, if appropriately restricted, construct all and only most-perfect squares. To test which, if any, method might be suitable, the 10 sets of most-perfect 8 by 8 squares, listed in Ollerenshaw (1986), have been inspected to see whether they could be constructed by using these methods. One such square is shown in Figure 1.5.1, with integers in octal.

$$
\begin{array}{cccc|cccc}
0 & 76 & 2 & 74 & 13 & 65 & 11 & 67 \\
17 & 61 & 15 & 63 & 4 & 72 & 6 & 70 \\
20 & 56 & 22 & 54 & 33 & 45 & 31 & 47 \\
37 & 41 & 35 & 43 & 24 & 52 & 26 & 50 \\
\hline
& - & & + & & - & \\
64 & 12 & 66 & 10 & 77 & 1 & 75 & 3 \\
73 & 5 & 71 & 7 & 60 & 16 & 62 & 14 \\
44 & 32 & 46 & 30 & 57 & 21 & 55 & 23 \\
53 & 25 & 51 & 27 & 40 & 36 & 42 & 34 \\
\end{array}
$$

Figure 1.5.1 An 8 by 8 most-perfect square
from Ollerenshaw (1986), in octal.

Consider whether or not the ten sets of 8 by 8 most-perfect squares can be constructed by using each of the methods from Section 1.3, in turn:

(i) The pair of auxiliary squares corresponding to the radix and the unit value of each integer in all the 8 by 8 most-perfect squares are not

Latin. For example, in Figure 1.5.1 the rows of the radix auxiliary and the columns of the units auxiliary each contain two copies of four digits. Hence Euler's method is not suitable.

(ii) These same auxiliary squares cannot be made by using paths (Frost's method) as the order in which the integers appear in each row/column is not the same (Appendix C.1.5). For example, in Figure 1.5.1 the radix digits in column 0 are, in order, 0, 1, 2, 3, 6, 7, 4, 5 but in column 4 the order is 1, 0, 3, 2, 7, 6, 5, 4.

(iii) The method of knight's paths in mixed auxiliary squares (Bellew, 1997) cannot be used to construct some of the 8 by 8 most-perfect squares, including the square in Figure 1.5.1 – see Appendix C.2.

(iv) The method of primitive squares (Rosser and Walker, 1939) can construct all the ten sets of 8 by 8 most-perfect squares. If the integers in the right half of each row and the bottom half of each column of a normalized primitive square are reversed, as illustrated in Figure 1.5.2 with integers in octal, then the resulting square, which is still primitive, can be transformed into a most-perfect square by using the transform

$$T = \begin{bmatrix} 1 & 4 \\ 4 & 5 \end{bmatrix}$$

i.e. the integer at position (i, j) goes to position $(i + 4j, 4i + 5j)$. Applying this transform to Figure 1.5.2*b* gives the most-perfect square of Figure 1.5.1.

(*a*) Normalized primitive square   (*b*) Reversed primitive square

0	1	2	3	10	11	12	13
4	5	6	7	14	15	16	17
20	21	22	23	30	31	32	33
24	25	26	27	34	35	36	37
40	41	42	43	50	51	52	53
44	45	46	47	54	55	56	57
60	61	62	63	70	71	72	73
64	65	66	67	74	75	76	77

0	1	2	3	13	12	11	10
4	5	6	7	17	16	15	14
20	21	22	23	33	32	31	30
24	25	26	27	37	36	35	34
64	65	66	67	77	76	75	74
60	61	62	63	73	72	71	70
44	45	46	47	57	56	55	54
40	41	42	43	53	52	51	50

Figure 1.5.2 An 8 by 8 normalized primitive square and its 'reversed' form, both in octal.

It is the method of primitive squares that will be adapted, with the use of ideas from McClintock squares, to generate a class of primitive squares, called 'reversible squares'. These then transform into most-perfect squares.[*]

[*] The development of the method of reversible squares actually arose out of McClintock squares rather than out of primitive squares – see the Personal perspective – but reversible squares are, in fact, a special case of primitive squares.

1.6 Overview

This chapter gives definitions and a brief history of magic squares, in particular of pandiagonal magic squares; and introduces the pandiagonal magic squares with additional properties that are here called most-perfect.

In Chapter 2, most-perfect squares and squares named **reversible** are defined. The definitions of **similar sequences** of integers and of **reverse similarity** necessary for defining reversible squares, are given here. The integers in all rows and in all columns of a reversible square consist of similar sequences of integers, all of which have a reverse similarity when reflected in their mid-point. Reversible squares can be grouped into sets, each set being uniquely represented by a **principal reversible square**. The integers in each row and column of a principal reversible square are in ascending order, the top row starting with 0 1. **Legitimate transformations** relate any reversible square within a set to all other reversible squares within the same set. The number of essentially different squares in each set depends only on the order of the square, so enumerating the number of principal reversible squares enables the total of all doubly-even reversible squares to be found.

Chapter 3 establishes that reversible squares of doubly-even order and most-perfect squares of the same order can be transformed one into the other. These transformations are defined and proved to lead to a one-to-one correspondence between squares of the two types. This concludes the discussion of the nature and structure of most-perfect squares; a method of construction and of enumeration of all principal reversible squares of doubly-even order follow in subsequent chapters.

Chapter 4 establishes that a principal reversible square of even order can always be exactly divided into similar rectangular **blocks** and blocks within blocks – of rows and columns that also consist of similar sequences of integers arranged in ascending order. In particular, there is always a **largest corner block** lying in the top left of the square with its corners at $(0,0)$, $(0, f - 1), (n - 1, f - 1), (n - 1,0)$. This block consists of the nf integers 0 to $(nf - 1)$ arranged in n similar rows and f similar columns with $1 < f \leq n$. It is proved that the conditions defining principal reversible squares in Chapter 2 ensure that f must be a factor of n. In general, there will be more than one possible arrangment of the ascending integers forming the rows and columns of a largest corner block; that is to say, a largest corner block may have a variety of different **configurations**.

The ensuing task, undertaken in Chapter 5, is to emumerate all possible different configurations for the largest corner block, for any given value of f that is a factor of $n = 2^r p^s$ (p any prime > 2; $r > 1$, $s > 0$ integers). The enumeration depends on finding the number of ways in which v **progressive**

(iii) *P* is of doubly-even order:

$$n \text{ modulo } 4 = 0. \tag{2.2.1.3}$$

Note that the subscripts of *p* are taken MODULO *n*. For instance in (2.2.1.1), if $i = (n - 1)$, then $(i + 1) = n$ modulo $n = 0$, and in (2.2.1.2), if $i > \frac{1}{2}n$, then $(i + \frac{1}{2}n) = (i + \frac{1}{2}n)$ modulo $n = (i - \frac{1}{2}n)$. Note also that most-perfect squares are shown to be pandiagonal and that pandiagonal squares are of doubly-even order (Section 1.3.3); hence most-perfect squares must be of doubly-even order.[*]

2.2.2 Most-perfect squares are pandiagonal magic squares

It is now shown that squares that satisfy (i), (ii) and (iii) above are pandiagonal, i.e. the sum of the integers in any row, in any column and in all diagonals (including broken diagonals) is the same, namely $\frac{1}{2}nS$. It is convenient to establish beforehand both that the sums of integers in alternate rows are equal and that, likewise, the sums of the integers in alternate columns are equal.

Let R_i, C_j denote the sums of the integers in any row *i*, column *j*, respectively:

$$R_i = \sum_{0 \le j < n} r_{i,j} \quad \text{for any } i,$$

$$C_j = \sum_{0 \le i < n} r_{i,j} \quad \text{for any } j.$$

EVEN/ODD rows are rows for which *i* is even/odd, respectively; EVEN/ODD COLUMNS are columns for which *j* is even/odd, respectively. Consider the $\frac{1}{2}n$ 2×2 arrays of integers that make up two adjacent rows $(i - 1)$ and *i*. They each sum to $2S$, so

$$R_{i-1} + R_i = nS \quad \text{by (2.2.1.1)}.$$

Likewise,

$$R_i + R_{i+1} = nS \quad \text{by (2.2.1.1)}.$$

Subtraction gives

$$R_{i-1} = R_{i+1} \quad \text{for all } i.$$

So,

$$R_i = R_{i+2h} \quad \text{for all } i \text{ and all integers } h,$$

---

[*] Most-perfect squares could have been defined as being pandiagonal, but neither (i) nor (ii) are characteristics of pandiagonal squares. Moreover, to prove that a square of doubly-even order is most-perfect it is only necessary to prove that it satisfies (i) and (ii), then it is also pandiagonal. This is the reason for our choice of the form of the definition.

where the subscripts are modulo n. Likewise, by considering the $\frac{1}{2}n$ 2 × 2 arrays that make up two adjacent columns, and so on,

$$C_j = C_{j+2h} \quad \text{for all } j \text{ and all integers } h.$$

Hence, all even rows/columns have the same sum and all odd rows/columns have the same sum. It is now shown that these sums are equal.

Consider two rows distant $\frac{1}{2}n$ apart. Each of the integers in the upper row is paired with an integer in the lower row, distant $\frac{1}{2}n$ along the row. These n pairs are S-complements. Hence the sum of the two rows is nS:

$$R_i + R_{i+\frac{1}{2}n} = nS \quad \text{by (2.2.1.2)}.$$

But it has just been shown that

$$R_i = R_{i+\frac{1}{2}n}$$

as $\frac{1}{2}n$ is even (n is a multiple of 4). Hence:

$$R_i = \tfrac{1}{2}nS \quad \text{for all } i.$$

Likewise, it can be shown that

$$C_j = \tfrac{1}{2}nS \quad \text{for all } j.$$

Hence:

(i) all rows have equal sums:

$$\sum_{0 \le j < n} p_{i,j} = \tfrac{1}{2}nS \quad \text{for all } i; \tag{2.2.2.1}$$

(ii) all columns have equal sums:

$$\sum_{0 \le i < n} p_{i,j} = \tfrac{1}{2}nS \quad \text{for all } j. \tag{2.2.2.2}$$

Consider now any diagonal. Each element in the top half of the diagonal is paired with the element distant $\frac{1}{2}n$ along its length. Each of these $\frac{1}{2}n$ pairs are S-complements by (2.2.1.2). Hence:

(iii) all diagonals have equal sums:

$$\sum_{0 \le i < n} p_{i,i+h} = \tfrac{1}{2}nS \quad \text{for all integers } h, \tag{2.2.2.3}$$

where $i + h$ is modulo n.

2.2.3 Additional characteristic of most-perfect squares

Most-perfect squares have characteristics other than those by which they are defined and that of being pandiagonal. One of these is useful in proving that any most-perfect square can be transformed into a reversible square of doubly-even order.

The characteristic is that two integers distant $\frac{1}{2}n$ along any row, with the left integer in an even column, have the same sum. The same is true when the left integer is in an odd column. These two sums (i.e. for evens and for odds) add to $2S$.

$$\left.\begin{aligned}
p_{i,0} + p_{i,\frac{1}{2}n} &= p_{i,2j} + p_{i,2j+\frac{1}{2}n} \\
p_{i,1} + p_{i,1+\frac{1}{2}n} &= p_{i,2j+1} + p_{i,2j+1+\frac{1}{2}n} \\
p_{i,0} + p_{i,\frac{1}{2}n} + p_{i,1} + p_{i,1+\frac{1}{2}n} &= 2S
\end{aligned}\right\} \quad \text{for all } i, j. \tag{2.2.3.1}$$

Likewise, for two integers distant $\frac{1}{2}n$ along any column:

$$\left.\begin{aligned}
p_{0,j} + p_{\frac{1}{2}n,j} &= p_{2i,j} + p_{2i+\frac{1}{2}n,j} \\
p_{1,j} + p_{1+\frac{1}{2}n,j} &= p_{2i+1,j} + p_{2i+1+\frac{1}{2}n,j} \\
p_{0,j} + p_{\frac{1}{2}n,j} + p_{1,j} + p_{1+\frac{1}{2}n,j} &= 2S
\end{aligned}\right\} \quad \text{for all } i, j. \tag{2.2.3.2}$$

Note that a HORIZONTAL COUPLET of adjacent integers in the right half of a row are both S-complements of a horizontal couplet of integers in the left half of a row $\frac{1}{2}n$ down (or up) and that this complementary couplet is in adjacent columns distant $\frac{1}{2}n$ from the original couplet. Now the sum of the complementary couplet is the same as the sum of a horizontal couplet in the same columns, but in a row $\frac{1}{2}n$ up (or down), i.e. in the original row. Hence, the sum of any horizontal couplet, plus the sum of the horizontal couplet distant $\frac{1}{2}n$ along the same row, is $2S$. By taking two such couplets with one element in common, the proof of (2.2.3.1) follows. The proof of (2.2.3.2) for columns proceeds likewise. The proofs can be found in Appendix B.2.

2.3 Reversible squares

After defining similarity and reverse similarity between sequences of integers (Section 2.3.1), these terms are used to define reversible squares (Section 2.3.2). Some significant additional characteristics of reversible squares are then derived (Section 2.3.3). An example of a reversible square is given in Figure 2.3.

2.3.1 Similarity and reverse similarity

Central to the definition of reversible squares is the 'similarity' and the 'reverse similarity' of sequences of integers. Two sequences of equal length, say h, consisting of integers $a_0, a_1, a_2, \ldots, a_{h-1}$ and $b_0, b_1, b_2, \ldots, b_{h-1}$, are said to be SIMILAR when the difference between the two integers at the same position in each sequence is constant, i.e. when

$$a_i - b_i = a_j - b_j \quad \text{for all } i, j, \quad 0 \le \{i, j\} < h.$$

From this follows the property of EQUAL CROSS SUMS:

$$a_i + b_j = a_j + b_i \quad \text{for all } i, j, \quad 0 \le \{i, j\} < h.$$

The two sequences are said to be in REVERSE SIMILARITY when, if the second

64	51	81	49	48	66	65	83	82	50	80	67
28	15	45	13	12	30	29	47	46	14	44	31
24	11	41	9	8	26	25	43	42	10	40	27
20	7	37	5	4	22	21	39	38	6	36	23
16	3	33	1	0	18	17	35	34	2	32	19
72	59	89	57	56	74	73	91	90	58	88	75

$+$

68	55	85	53	52	70	69	87	86	54	84	71
124	111	141	109	108	126	125	143	142	110	140	127
120	107	137	105	104	122	121	139	138	106	136	123
116	103	133	101	100	118	117	135	134	102	132	119
112	99	129	97	96	114	113	131	130	98	128	115
76	63	93	61	60	78	77	95	94	62	92	79

Figure 2.3 A reversible square of order 12.

sequence is reversed, the **sum** of pairs of integers in the same position in each sequence is constant, i.e.

$$a_i + b_{h-1-i} = a_j + b_{h-1-j} \quad \text{for all } i, j, \ 0 \le \{i, j\} < h.$$

For example, if the a's are 1 2 3 4 ' 8 9 and the b's are 11 12 ' 16 17 18 19, which in reverse are 19 18 17 16 ' 12 11, this gives a reverse similarity to the a's: the a's added to the reversed b's give here the constant 20.

2.3.2 Defining reversible squares

With the definitions of similarity and reverse similarity of sequences of integers given above, the square R is a REVERSIBLE SQUARE if it contains the n^2 consecutive integers 0 to $(n^2 - 1)$ and:

   (i) the left-hand and right-hand halves of each row have reverse similarity;
   (ii) the top and bottom halves of each column have reverse similarity;
   (iii) in any rectangular array of integers within the square, the sums of integers in opposite corners are equal.

Let $r_{i,j}$ be the element in row i, column j, $0 \le \{i, j\} < n$, of an n by n square, R, of consecutive integers 0 to $(n^2 - 1)$. The square is thus reversible if and only if:

   (i) the rows have reverse similarity:

$$r_{i,j} + r_{i,n-1-j} = r_{i,j'} + r_{i,n-1-j'} \quad \text{for any } i, j, j'; \tag{2.3.2.1}$$

   (ii) the columns have reverse similarity:

$$r_{i,j} + r_{n-1-i,j} = r_{i',j} + r_{n-1-i',j} \quad \text{for any } i, i', j; \tag{2.3.2.2}$$

(iii) arrays have equal cross sums at their corners:

$$r_{i,j} + r_{i',j'} = r_{i,j'} + r_{i',j} \quad \text{for any } i,\ i',\ j,\ j'. \tag{2.3.2.3}$$

By (2.3.2.3) reversible squares are a special case of Rosser and Walker's (1939) primitive squares.

2.3.3 Characteristics of reversible squares

Aside from their definitions, reversible squares have the following characteristics:

(i) The rows are similar:

$$r_{i,j} - r_{i,j'} = r_{i',j} - r_{i',j'} \quad \text{for any } i,\ i',\ j,\ j'. \tag{2.3.3.1}$$

This follows directly from (2.3.2.3) and vice versa.

(ii) The columns are similar:

$$r_{i,j} - r_{i',j} = r_{i,j'} - r_{i',j'} \quad \text{for any } i,\ i',\ j,\ j'. \tag{2.3.3.2}$$

This also follows directly from (2.3.2.3) and vice-versa.

(iii) The integers 0 and 1 must lie in the same row or column.   (2.3.3.3)
Because no two different positive integers, other than 0 and 1, can add to 1, there cannot be an array in which 0 and 1 are at opposite corners (2.3.2.3). Hence, 0 and 1 must lie in the same row or in the same column. Likewise, this is also true for the integers $(n^2 - 1)$ and $(n^2 - 2)$.

(iv) The pair of integers reflected in the mid-point of the square are S-complements:

$$r_{i,j} + r_{n-1-i,\,n-1-j} = S = (n^2 - 1) \quad \text{for any } i,\ j. \tag{2.3.3.4}$$

The proof is given in Appendix B.3.

(v) The sum of the integers in the principal diagonals and in the broken diagonals is the same $(\tfrac{1}{2}nS)$:

$$\sum_{0 \le i < n} r_{i,\,i+h} = \tfrac{1}{2}nS \quad \text{for all integers } h, \tag{2.3.3.5}$$

where $i + h$ is modulo n. This follows directly from (2.3.3.4).

By (2.3.3.4), the top left and bottom right quarter squares of a reversible square of even order consist of S-complementary integers, as do the top right and bottom left quarter squares. It follows that no row or column can contain S-complementary integers.

2.4 Transformations of reversible squares that lead to other reversible squares

Reversible squares can be subject to certain transformations while still remaining reversible. These 'legitimate' transformations are defined in Section 2.4.1. Some lead to new reversible squares that should not be considered to be essentially different; others lead to squares that should be considered essentially different and counted as such. Essentially different reversible squares that can be legitimately transformed into each other form sets of constant size M_n (Section 2.4.2).

2.4.1 Legitimate transformations

Let $q_{i,j}$ be the elements of a square created by a transformation applied to a reversible square R, with elements $r_{i,j}$. The legitimate transformations of reversible squares that lead to other reversible squares are:

(i) reflection about the vertical axis:

$$q_{i,j} = r_{i,n-1-j} \quad \text{for all } i, j; \qquad (2.4.1.1)$$

(ii) reflection about the horizontal axis:

$$q_{i,j} = r_{n-1-i,j} \quad \text{for all } i, j; \qquad (2.4.1.2)$$

(iii) reflection about either principal diagonal:

$$q_{i,j} = r_{j,i}, \qquad (2.4.1.3)$$

$$q_{i,j} = r_{n-1-j,n-1-i} \quad \text{for all } i, j; \qquad (2.4.1.4)$$

(iv) interchanging complementary pairs of rows:

$$\left. \begin{array}{l} q_{i',j} = r_{n-1-i',j} \\ q_{n-1-i',j} = r_{i',j} \end{array} \right\} \quad \text{for all } j, \text{ and for any one value of } i';$$

$$q_{i,j} = r_{i,j} \quad \text{for all } i, j, \; i \neq \{i', (n - i')\}; \qquad (2.4.1.5)$$

(v) interchanging complementary pairs of columns:

$$\left. \begin{array}{l} q_{i,j'} = r_{i,n-1-j'} \\ q_{i,n-1-j'} = r_{i,j'} \end{array} \right\} \quad \text{for all } i, \text{ and for any one value of } j';$$

$$q_{i,j} = r_{i,j} \text{ for all } i, j, \; j \neq \{j', (n - 1 - j')\}; \qquad (2.4.1.6)$$

(vi) interchanging a pair of rows, i' and i'', in one half of the square and, at the same time, interchanging the pair of rows in the other half of the square that are the complements of the first pair:

$$\left. \begin{array}{l} q_{i',j} = r_{i'',j} \\ q_{i'',j} = r_{i',j} \\ q_{n-1-i',j} = r_{n-1-i'',j} \\ q_{n-1-i'',j} = r_{n-1-i',j} \end{array} \right\} \quad \begin{array}{l} \text{for all } j, \text{ and} \\ \text{unique } i' \text{ and } i'', \; 0 \leq \{i', i''\} < \tfrac{1}{2}n \end{array}$$

$$q_{i,j} = r_{i,j} \quad \text{for all } i, j, \text{ such that}$$
$$i \neq \{i', i'', (n - 1 - i'), (n - 1 - i'')\}; \qquad (2.4.1.7)$$

(vii) interchanging a pair of columns, j' and j'', in one half of the square and, at the same time, interchanging the pair of columns in the other half of the square that are the complements of the first pair:

$$q_{i,j'} = r_{i,j''}$$
$$q_{i,j''} = r_{i,j'}$$
$$q_{i,n-1-j'} = r_{i,n-1-j''} \quad \text{for all } i, \text{ and}$$
$$q_{i,n-1-j''} = r_{i,n-1-j'} \quad \text{unique } j' \text{ and } j'', \ 0 \leq \{j', j''\} < \tfrac{1}{2}n$$

$$q_{i,j} = r_{i,j} \quad \text{for all } i, j, \text{ such that}$$
$$j \neq \{j', j'', (n-1-j'), (n-1-j'')\}. \tag{2.4.1.8}$$

The proofs that each of these transformations lead to reversible squares are given in Appendix B.4.

2.4.2 Sets of reversible squares

Define as a SET OF REVERSIBLE SQUARES those that can be transformed into one another by any combination of the legitimate transformations. Legitimate transformations are of two kinds: those that do not lead to essentially different squares, and those that do. By definition, squares that cannot be transformed one into the other by reflections in the vertical or horizontal axis or in either of the principal diagonals are ESSENTIALLY DIFFERENT.

Only four of the legitimate transformations lead to an essentially different reversible square:

(i) interchanging a pair of complementary rows/columns,
(ii) interchanging two rows/columns in one half of the square together with interchanging the complementary rows/columns in the other half of the square.

To determine how many essentially different squares there are in a set, note that, since n is even, interchanging columns enables any column of integers to be moved to a given position. There are therefore n ways of choosing the leftmost column, i.e. column 0. This fixes the integers in its complementary column $(n-1)$. There remain $(n-2)$ ways of choosing the next column, column 1, which fixes the integers in column $(n-2)$, and so on. Therefore, as n is even, the number of ways of arranging the columns is:

$$n(n-2)(n-4) \ldots \left[n - 2\left(\tfrac{1}{2}n - 1\right)\right] = \tfrac{1}{2}n\left(\tfrac{1}{2}n - 1\right)\left(\tfrac{1}{2}n - 2\right) \ldots \times$$
$$\times \left(\tfrac{1}{2}n - \tfrac{1}{2}n + 1\right) 2^{\frac{1}{2}n}$$
$$= \left(\tfrac{1}{2}n\right)! \, 2^{\frac{1}{2}n}.$$

But these arrangements come in pairs that are reflections about the vertical axis and so are not essentially different. Hence, the number of essentially different reversible squares of even order obtained by interchanging columns is $\left(\tfrac{1}{2}n\right)! \, 2^{\frac{1}{2}n - 1}$.

Likewise, the number of essentially different reversible squares of even order obtained by interchanging rows is $\left(\tfrac{1}{2}n\right)! \, 2^{\frac{1}{2}n - 1}$. The total number of essentially different squares that can be reached from one reversible square of even order is thus

$$M_n = \left\{2^{\frac{1}{2}n-1}\left(\tfrac{1}{2}n\right)!\right\}^2 = 2^{n-2}\left\{\left(\tfrac{1}{2}n\right)!\right\}^2. \qquad (2.4.2.1)$$

The total number of essentially different reversible squares of even order is now given by the product of M_n and the number of sets, N_n.

2.4.3 A set of essentially different squares with $n = 4$

By way of illustration, a particular complete set of essentially different reversible squares with $n = 4$ is shown in Figure 2.4.3. Note that the four squares in any one row of Figure 2.4.3 can be reached from each other by interchanging complementary rows, or a couple of rows in one half and their complementary rows in the other half of the square. The four squares in any one column of the figure can be reached from each other likewise, by interchanging columns.

```
 0  1  2  3     0  1  2  3     4  5  6  7     4  5  6  7
 4  5  6  7     8  9 10 11     0  1  2  3    12 13 14 15
 8  9 10 11     4  5  6  7    12 13 14 15     0  1  2  3
12 13 14 15    12 13 14 15     8  9 10 11     8  9 10 11

 0  2  1  3     0  2  1  3     4  6  5  7     4  6  5  7
 4  6  5  7     8 10  9 11     0  2  1  3    12 14 13 15
 8 10  9 11     4  6  5  7    12 14 13 15     0  2  1  3
12 14 13 15    12 14 13 15     8 10  9 11     8 10  9 11

 1  0  3  2     1  0  3  2     5  4  7  6     5  4  7  6
 5  4  7  6     9  8 11 10     1  0  3  2    13 12 15 14
 9  8 11 10     5  4  7  6    13 12 15 14     1  0  3  2
13 12 15 14    13 12 15 14     9  8 11 10     9  8 11 10

 1  3  0  2     1  3  0  2     5  7  4  6     5  7  4  6
 5  7  4  6     9 11  8 10     1  3  0  2    13 15 12 14
 9 11  8 10     5  7  4  6    13 15 12 14     1  3  0  2
13 15 12 14    13 15 12 14     9 11  8 10     9 11  8 10
```

Figure 2.4.3 A set of essentially different reversible squares with $n = 4$.

In the next section it is shown that any even-ordered reversible square can be rearranged into a canonical form, called a 'principal reversible square', by using only legitimate transformations. The 4 by 4 principal reversible square in Figure 2.4.3 is the leftmost square in the top row of squares.

Reversible squares of even order can be grouped into sets, each set characterized by its principal reversible square and containing M_n essentially different reversible squares.

3

Mapping between most-perfect and doubly-even reversible squares

To construct a most-perfect square from a reversible square of doubly-even order, there must be a means of transforming any such doubly-even reversible square into a most-perfect square. A transform that does this is specified in Section 3.1.1. To use the enumeration of doubly-even reversible squares as a count of most-perfect squares, it must be established not only that every doubly-even reversible square can be transformed into a most-perfect square (Section 3.1), but also that every most-perfect square can be derived from a reversible square (Section 3.2), i.e. that there is a one-to-one correspondence between doubly-even reversible and most-perfect squares.

3.1 Transforming a doubly-even reversible square into a most-perfect square

The method of transforming a doubly-even reversible square into a most-perfect square is now given, and a one-to-one mapping from doubly-even reversible squares to most-perfect squares is established.

3.1.1 The transformation

Consider the doubly-even reversible square R of order n, n modulo $4 = 0$, composed of elements $r_{i,j}$ in row i and column j, $0 \leq \{i, j\} < n$. To TRANSFORM this square into a most-perfect square:

    (i) reverse the right-hand half of each row;
    (ii) reverse the bottom half of each column;
    (iii) apply the transform[*]

$$T = \begin{bmatrix} 1 & k \\ k & k+1 \end{bmatrix}, \quad \text{where } k = \tfrac{1}{2}n. \tag{3.1.1.1}$$

---

[*] This transform is a special case of the transform (1.3.5.1) used in the method of primitive squares developed by Rosser and Walker (1939).

[33]

The effect of applying T can also be achieved by:
- interchanging the top and bottom halves of odd columns (the effect of the top row of T);
- in even rows, interchanging all pairs of integers distant k in odd columns;
- in odd rows, interchanging all pairs of integers distant k in even columns.

Let the result of applying steps (i) and (ii) to R be the intermediary square Q of order n with elements

$$q_{i,j} = \begin{cases} r_{i,j} & \text{for } i < k,\ j < k; \\ r_{i,\,3k-1-j} & \text{for } i < k,\ j \ge k; \\ r_{3k-1-i,\,j} & \text{for } i \ge k,\ j < k; \\ r_{3k-1-i,\,3k-1-j} & \text{for } i \ge k,\ j \ge k. \end{cases} \tag{3.1.1.2}$$

At step (iii) the result of applying T to all the vectors $q = \left[\begin{smallmatrix}i\\j\end{smallmatrix}\right]$, corresponding to the elements $q_{i,j}$ in Q, are the vectors p such that

$$p = Tq = \begin{bmatrix} 1 & k \\ k & 1+k \end{bmatrix}\begin{bmatrix} i \\ j \end{bmatrix} = \begin{bmatrix} i + kj \\ ki + (1+k)j \end{bmatrix}.$$

Each vector p gives the position in a square P at which the element at (i, j) in Q is placed. Note that $q = T^{-1}p$, where T^{-1} is the inverse of T:

$$T^{-1} = \begin{bmatrix} (1+k)\varepsilon & -k\varepsilon \\ -k\varepsilon & \varepsilon \end{bmatrix}, \quad \text{where } \varepsilon\,(1 + k - k^2) \text{ modulo } n = 1.$$

As $k^2 = \tfrac{1}{4}n^2$ and n modulo $4 = 0$, k^2 modulo $n = 0$. Therefore $\varepsilon = (1 - k)$ and

$$T^{-1} = \begin{bmatrix} 1 - k^2 & -k(1-k) \\ -k(1-k) & 1-k \end{bmatrix} = \begin{bmatrix} 1 & -k \\ -k & 1-k \end{bmatrix} = \begin{bmatrix} 1 & k \\ k & 1+k \end{bmatrix} \tag{3.1.1.3}$$

as subscripts are taken modulo n. Note that $T = T^{-1}$ but that even so TT^{-1} modulo $n = I$, the identity matrix, as required. Therefore the elements of P are

$$p_{i,j} = q_{i+kj,\,ki+(1+k)j} = q_{i+jk,\,j+(i+j)k}. \tag{3.1.1.4}$$

Combining all three steps, the complete transformation of R results in a square P with elements $p_{i,j} = r_{I,J}$, where

$$I = \begin{cases} i + jk & \text{for } i < k \text{ and } j \text{ even or } i \ge k \text{ and } j \text{ odd}, \\ -(i+1) + (3-j)k & \text{otherwise}; \end{cases}$$

$$J = \begin{cases} j + (i+j)k & \text{for } j < k \text{ and } (i+j) \text{ even or} \\ & \qquad j \ge k \text{ and } (i+j) \text{ odd}, \\ -(j+1) + (3-i-j)k & \text{otherwise}. \end{cases} \tag{3.1.1.5}$$

As a simple illustration, consider these steps applied to a 4 by 4 principal reversible square, as shown in Figure 3.1.1, using integers expressed to the base 4, with the final square in decimal.

$$
\begin{array}{ccccc}
R & & & & Q \\
\end{array}
$$

R			(i)	Q				(ii)				

R						(i)					(ii)			

$$
\begin{array}{l}
\qquad R \qquad\qquad\qquad\qquad\qquad\qquad\qquad Q \\
\begin{array}{cccc}
0 & 1 & 2 & 3 \\
10 & 11 & 12 & 13 \\
20 & 21 & 22 & 23 \\
30 & 31 & 32 & 33
\end{array}
\quad (i) \quad
\begin{array}{cccc}
0 & 1 & 3 & 2 \\
10 & 11 & 13 & 12 \\
20 & 21 & 23 & 22 \\
30 & 31 & 33 & 32
\end{array}
\quad (ii) \quad
\begin{array}{cccc}
0 & 1 & 3 & 2 \\
10 & 11 & 13 & 12 \\
30 & 31 & 33 & 32 \\
20 & 21 & 23 & 22
\end{array}
\end{array}
$$

$$
\begin{array}{ll}
P \text{ (to the base 4)} & P \text{ (decimal)} \\
\begin{array}{cccc}
0 & 32 & 3 & 31 \\
13 & 21 & 10 & 22 \\
30 & 2 & 33 & 1 \\
23 & 11 & 20 & 12
\end{array}
& =
\begin{array}{cccc}
0 & 14 & 3 & 13 \\
7 & 9 & 4 & 10 \\
12 & 2 & 15 & 1 \\
11 & 5 & 8 & 6
\end{array}
\end{array}
$$

(iii) appears before the base-4 P square.

Figure 3.1.1 Transforming a 4 by 4 reversible square R into a most-perfect square P.

3.1.2 The transformation leads to a unique most-perfect square

The transformation (3.1.1.5) applied to any different reversible square R clearly leads to a different square P. To show that P is a most-perfect square, it must be shown that the sum of any 2×2 array is $2S$, which is (2.2.1.1), and that any pair of integers distant k along any diagonal sum to $S = (n^2 - 1)$, which is (2.2.1.2). To prove that this is so, two characteristics of the intermediary square Q are first established.

Any array in a reversible square R has by definition equal cross sums (2.3.2.3). Interchanging rows or interchanging columns does not alter this characteristic (Appendix B.4.5 and B.4.6). Hence any array within the square Q has equal cross sums, i.e. it is also a primitive square. Secondly, any pair of integers in the square distant k along a diagonal sum to S, as they are always taken from positions in the reversible square that are reflections about its mid-point (2.3.3.4):

$$
q_{i,j} + q_{i+k,\,j+k} =
\begin{cases}
r_{i,j} & + r_{n-1-i,\,n-1-j} = S, & \text{for } i < k,\ j < k; \\
r_{i,\,3k-1-j} & + r_{n-1-i,\,j+k} = S, & \text{for } i < k,\ j \ge k; \\
r_{3k-1-i,\,j} & + r_{i+k,\,n-1-j} = S, & \text{for } i \ge k,\ j < k; \\
r_{3k-1-i,\,3k-1-j} & + r_{i+k,\,j+k} = S, & \text{for } i \ge k,\ j \ge k.
\end{cases}
$$

That is to say, $\qquad q_{i,j} + q_{i+k,\,j+k} = S.$ $\qquad\qquad\qquad\qquad$ (3.1.2.1)

Turn now to proving that P is a most-perfect square and let

$$
I = i + jk, \qquad J = j + (i + j)k.
$$

The four integers in any 2×2 array in P are, by (3.1.1.3):

$$p_{i,j} = q_{i+jk,\,j+(i+j)k} = q_{I,J};$$
$$p_{i,j+1} = q_{I+k,\,J+k+1} = S - q_{I,J+1} \quad \text{by (3.1.2.1)};$$
$$p_{i+1,j} = q_{I+1,\,J+k} = S - q_{I+1+k,\,J} \quad \text{by (3.1.2.1)};$$
$$p_{i+1,j+1} = q_{I+1+k,\,J+2k+1} = q_{I+1+k,\,J+1}.$$

Adding these four integers and noting that, as Q is a primitive square,

$$q_{I,J} + q_{I+1+k,\,J+1} = q_{I,J+1} + q_{I+1+k,\,J},$$

gives: $\qquad p_{i,j} + p_{i,j+1} + p_{i+1,j} + p_{i+1,j+1} = 2S,$

i.e. the square P satisfies (2.2.1.1).

Also the sum of any pair of integers distant k along a diagonal of P is:

$$p_{i,j} + p_{i+k,\,j+k} = q_{I,J} + q_{I+k+k^2,\,J+k+2k^2}$$
$$= q_{I,J} + q_{I+k,\,J+k}, \qquad \text{as } k^2 \text{ modulo } n = 0$$
$$= S, \qquad\qquad\qquad \text{by (3.1.2.1)},$$

and so the square P satisfies (2.2.1.2).

P satisfies both (2.2.1.1) and (2.2.1.2) and so is a most-perfect square. It follows that there is a one-to-one mapping from any doubly-even reversible square to a most-perfect square.

3.2 Every most-perfect square can be reached from a reversible square

To establish a one-to-one correspondence **between** doubly-even reversible squares and most-perfect squares it has also to be shown that every different most-perfect square is transformed into a different reversible square by the inverse of the transformation defined in (3.1.1.5).

3.2.1 The inverse transformation

The INVERSE TRANSFORMATION is simply the steps (i) to (iii) of the original transformation (Section 3.1.1) applied in reverse, i.e. apply T^{-1}, the inverse of T, to a most-perfect square P to give an intermediary square Q and then reverse the bottom half of each column and the right half of each row to give a square R. That is to say:

(i) apply the inverse of T, which is (3.1.1.3)

$$T^{-1} = \begin{bmatrix} 1 & k \\ k & 1+k \end{bmatrix}; \qquad\qquad (3.2.1.1)$$

(ii) reverse the bottom half of each column;

(iii) reverse the right-hand half of each row.

corner block, they will cover the depth of the square exactly if and only if n_v is a factor of n. Hence, if f_v and n_v are both factors of n, then the square can be exactly covered by blocks similar to $B_0 (n_v, f_v)$ placed in 'layers' of depth n_v rows across its full width.

The block $B_0 (n_v, f_v)$ may itself be divided into smaller similar rectangular blocks, say $B_{g'} (n_{v'}, f_{v'})$, provided there exist an $n_{v'}$ and an $f_{v'}$ that are factors of n_v and of f_v respectively.

4.1.4 The top row determines the entire square

It will be shown that a principal reversible square can be constructed by starting with a 'smallest corner block' (Section 4.3), using this to build larger corner blocks, until the 'largest corner block' is reached (Section 4.4). Then blocks similar to this largest corner block are arranged to cover the entire width of the square (Section 4.5).

This process, of constructing larger and larger corner blocks and then arranging blocks similar to the largest corner block along the top of the square, is the method used for selecting a top row. Once the top row, named row 0, of the square has been filled, the lowest integer that has not been used must be placed at the position (1,0), as there is nowhere else for it to go because the integers must be in ascending order. By row similarity, this determines the integers to be placed in row 1. The lowest remaining integer must then be placed at (2,0), which determines row 2, and so on. Thus, **once the top row is chosen, the rest of the square is determined**.

To base the method of construction of the top row on blocks, it must first be shown that **every** principal reversible square is composed of blocks similar to its smallest corner block (Section 4.2).

4.2 A principal reversible square must be constructed from similar blocks

In this section it is shown that a principal reversible square is always made up of blocks. First, it is shown that whenever there is a break in the sequence of consecutive integers in the top row, the first such break, reading from left to right, specifies a corner block, called the 'smallest corner block.' Blocks similar to this smallest corner block must then cover the top rows and the leftmost columns of the square. This, in turn, means that the whole square must be composed of blocks similar to the smallest corner block. In the unique principal reversible square with no break in the top row, i.e. in which the integers are arranged consecutively beginning with the top row, the entire square is taken to be the smallest corner block. So, all principal reversible squares are made up of blocks similar to the smallest corner block.

4.2.1 Gaps > 1 (if any)

By definition, the top row of the principal reversible square starts with 0 1 and contains n integers arranged in ascending order, read from left to right. When the difference between the ascending integers in the positions $(0, f_v - 1)$ and $(0, f_v)$, say, is > 1, this is defined as a GAP > 1. Reverse similarity of rows ensures that each gap > 1 in the left half of the top row is matched by an equal gap in the same relative position in the right half, read from right to left.

4.2.2 The first gap > 1 in the top row ensures that there is a smallest corner block

If there is a gap > 1 in the top row, let $(0, f_1)$ be the position after the first such gap. The integer that occurs at $(0, f_1)$ will be shown to be a multiple of f_1.

Consider an example in which $f_1 = 3$, and so the top row begins '0 1 2'. The smallest integer that can be placed at (0,3) is 6. For if 3 were to be put there, then there would be no gap > 1 before (0,3), contrary to the example. So 3 must be placed at (1,0), as otherwise there would be an integer > 3 either above it or to its left, contrary to the requirement of integers being placed in ascending order. By row similarity, row 1 must now begin '3 4 5'; hence 6 is the smallest integer that can be put at (0,3).

Assume that 6 is placed at (0,3), then, by column similarity, 9 must be put at (1,3). Consequently 7 and 8 must be placed on the top row as well. (Putting 7 at the only other possible position, (2,0), would result in row 2 beginning '7 8 9', but 9 has already been placed.) By row similarity, the top left of the square is now:

$$0 \quad 1 \quad 2 \qquad 6 \quad 7 \quad 8 \quad \ldots$$
$$3 \quad 4 \quad 5 \qquad 9 \quad 10 \quad 11 \quad \ldots \, .$$

If 6 is not placed at (0,3), then it must be placed at (2,0). Then, by row similarity, row 2 must begin '6 7 8'. Hence, the next highest integer that can be put at (0,3) is 9. Column similarity then requires column 3 to begin '9 12 15'. This in turn requires 10 and 11 to be placed on the top row, and then row similarity leads to:

$$0 \quad 1 \quad 2 \qquad 9 \quad 10 \quad 11 \quad \ldots$$
$$3 \quad 4 \quad 5 \qquad 12 \quad 13 \quad 14 \quad \ldots$$
$$6 \quad 7 \quad 8 \qquad 15 \quad 16 \quad 17 \quad \ldots \, .$$

Likewise, any other integer placed at (0,3) must be a factor of 3. So, in this example, there must be a smallest corner block $B_0\,(n_1, 3)$, where $1 < n_1 \leq n$, consisting of the $3n_1$ consecutive integers 0 to $3n_1 - 1$.

In general, if the first gap > 1 in the top row occurs immediately before the position $(0, f_1)$, the integer at $(0, f_1)$ must be an integral mutiple of f_1, as all the lesser integers must be placed consecutively in the leftmost f_1 positions in the required number, say n_1, $1 < n_1 \leq n$, of rows. Thus, when there is a first gap > 1 before the position $(0, f_1)$ in the top row, there must always be a SMALLEST CORNER BLOCK, $B_0(n_1, f_1)$. The rows of $B_0(n_1, f_1)$ consist, when taken from the top downward, of the consecutive integers 0 to $(f_1 - 1)$, f_1 to $(2f_1 - 1)$, ... , $(n_1 - 1)f_1$ to $(n_1 f_1 - 1)$, the differences between the integers in the leftmost column being f_1. **Also, the integer at the position $(0, f_1)$ must always be $n_1 f_1$.**

By column similarity, the top of column f_1 begins with the integers $n_1 f_1$, $(n_1 + 1)f_1$, ..., $(2n_1 - 1)f_1$. As $(n_1 + 1)f_1$ is at $(1, f_1)$, none of the integers $(n_1 f_1 + 1)$ to $(n_1 + 1)f_1 - 1$ can be placed in the leftmost column, nor in any of the other leftmost f_1 columns. Hence, they must be placed consecutively along the top row. By row similarity, the integers $< 2n_1 f_1$ that have not yet been allocated a position must be placed consecutively in the columns $(f_1 + 1)$ up to $(2f_1 - 1)$ of the rows 0 to n_1. Thus, a block $B_1(n_1, f_1)$ similar to the corner block $B_0(n_1, f_1)$, with the integer $n_1 f_1$ in its top-left corner, is completed.

4.2.3 The top n_1 rows must be filled with similar blocks

Now that blocks $B_0(n_1, f_1)$ and $B_1(n_1, f_1)$ have been placed side by side along the top of the square, there are two possibilities: either the top row is complete (which happens if $f_1 = \frac{1}{2}n$) or there is space in the top row for another integer to be placed at $(0, 2f_1)$.

Consider the example introduced in the previous section. Assume that the top row is not complete, so that another integer can be placed at $(0,6)$. Choose this integer to be 36. The eighteen integers 18 to 35 must now be placed in the next three rows of the leftmost six columns. By row similarity, this must be done in sequences of three consecutive integers. Here, as there are eighteen integers by appropriate choice, this can be done. Then, by column similarity, the three factors of 3, '36 39 42', must form the top of column 6. The integers 37 and 38 cannot be placed in the next three rows of the first six columns as 39 is already positioned; so they must be placed on the top row to the right of 36. Then the rest of the next 3 by 3 block must be completed by row similarity, to give:

$$
\begin{array}{ccc\quad ccc\quad ccc}
0 & 1 & 2 & 9 & 10 & 11 & 36 & 37 & 38 & \ldots \\
3 & 4 & 5 & 12 & 13 & 14 & 39 & 40 & 41 & \ldots \\
6 & 7 & 8 & 15 & 16 & 17 & 42 & 43 & 44 & \ldots \; .
\end{array}
$$

$$18 \quad 19 \quad 20 \qquad \ldots \qquad .$$

In general, the integer placed at $(0,2f_1)$, when this position exists, must also be an integral multiple of f_1. The consecutive integers from $2n_1 f_1$ up to this integer have to be placed in the first $2f_1$ columns, in sequences of f_1 consecutive integers, because of row similarity. This can be achieved only if there is an integral multiple of f_1 integers to be placed. Hence, the integer at the position $(0,2f_1)$ must be an integral multiple of f_1. Once this integer, say hf_1, has been placed at $(0,2f_1)$, then the top n_1 positions in column $2f_1$ must be filled, by column similarity, with the integers hf_1, $(h + 1)f_1$, $(h + 2)f_1$, ..., $(h + n_1 - 1)f_1$. As the integer $(h + 1)f_1$ is at $(1,2f_1)$, the integers $(hf_1 + 1)$, $(hf_1 + 2)$, ... $(h + 1)f_1 - 1$ must be placed along the top row to complete a sequence of f_1 consecutive integers, starting at $(0,2f_1)$. (There has to be space in the top row for this to be possible, i.e. $3f_1 \leq n$, otherwise no reversible square can be built.) By row similarity, there must then be a block similar to the smallest corner block with its top-left corner at $(0,2f_1)$.

In general, whenever the top row has been partly filled with two or more sequences of f_1 consecutive integers, each sequence always starting with an integral multiple of f_1, if $f_1 \leq \frac{1}{2}n$, then the next integer to be placed on the top row must always be an integral multiple of f_1 and it must be the first of a sequence of f_1 consecutive integers placed along the top row. So **the top row must consist of sequences of f_1 consecutive integers, each sequence starting with an integer that is an integral multiple of f_1.** The top row can be filled in this way only if f_1 is a factor of n. **There is no other way of filling the top row, so f_1 is a factor of n.**

By column similarity, the top n_1 integers in each column that is an integral multiple of f_1 must, after beginning with an integral multiple of f_1, be followed by the next $(n_1 - 1)$ integral multiples of f_1. Then, by row similarity, the next f_1 columns of the top n_1 rows must be filled with consecutive integers. In brief, the top n_1 rows must be covered by n/f_1 blocks similar to the smallest corner block, $B_0 (n_1, f_1)$.

4.2.4 The leftmost f_1 columns must be filled with similar blocks

In the example in the above section, suppose that the square is of order 12. Then the top three rows must, by reverse similarity of rows, be completed as follows:

0	1	2	9	10	11	36	37	38	45	46	47
3	4	5	12	13	14	39	40	41	48	49	50
6	7	8	15	16	17	42	43	44	51	52	53.

The integer 18 must then be placed at $(3,0)$, as there is nowhere else for it to go. By row similarity, row 3 is then determined as:

18	19	20	27	28	29	54	55	56	63	64	65.

The integers between 20 and 27 exclusive must now be used to complete a block similar to the smallest corner block, $B_0 (3,3)$. This, together with row similarity, gives the next three rows as:

18	19	20		27	28	29		54	55	56		63	64	65
21	22	23		30	31	32		57	58	59		66	67	68
24	25	26		33	34	35		60	61	62		69	70	71.

So, whenever a block similar to the smallest corner block, $B_0(3,3)$, has been placed going down the leftmost three columns, then a new row must begin with three consecutive integers and a new block similar to $B_0(3,3)$ must be completed.

In general, whenever the top n_1 rows have been completed, the smallest remaining integer must be placed at the position $(n_1,0)$. Then, by row similarity, this must start a new sequence of f_1 consecutive integers. The next largest integer cannot be placed at (n_1, f_1), because of row similarity with the top row; so it must go at $(n_1 + 1,0)$ and be the start of another sequence of f_1 consecutive integers. And so on, until the leftmost f_1 positions in the next n_1 rows are filled, forming another block similar to the smallest corner block, $B_0(n_1, f_1)$, with its top-left corner at $(n_1,0)$.

Therefore, provided that the top part of the leftmost f_1 columns has been filled with blocks similar to $B_0(n_1, f_1)$, the leftmost f_1 columns of the next n_1 rows must be filled with integers to form a new block similar to the smallest corner block, $B_0(n_1, f_1)$. The smallest corner block, $B_0(n_1, f_1)$, must always be placed in the top-left corner of the square, as has been shown above. Hence, **the leftmost f_1 columns must always be filled with blocks similar to $B_0(n_1, f_1)$, where n_1 must be a factor of n.**

4.2.5 The entire square must be filled with similar blocks

It has been shown that the top n_1 rows and the leftmost f_1 columns must both be covered by blocks similar to the smallest corner block, $B_0(n_1, f_1)$. By equal cross sums, the rest of **the square must also be filled with blocks similar to the smallest corner block. There is no other way to construct a principal reversible square with a gap > 1 in its top row.**

The questions arise both of how to arrange the blocks similar to $B_0(n_1, f_1)$ to form a principal reversible square, and of how many different ways there are of doing this. The first question will be answered in the remainder of this chapter. The rest of the book will be required to answer the second question.

4.3 The smallest corner block, $B_0(n_1, f_1)$

The smallest corner block $B_0(n_1, f_1)$, of depth n_1 partial rows and width f_1 partial columns, is completely defined by the **position** of the gap immediately before $(0, f_1)$, together with the **size** of the gap, namely $n_1 f_1 - (f_1 - 1)$. Two situations need to be distinguished, depending on whether or not there is a gap > 1 in the left half of the top row.

If there is no gap > 1 anywhere in the top row, then by decree the smallest corner block is $B_0(n, n)$, i.e. the whole square.

If the top row of the square does **not** consist of the consecutive integers 0 to $(n - 1)$, then there must be a gap > 1 between at least one pair of successive integers within this top row. Suppose that there is just one such gap. Then, for rows to have reverse similarity, the gap must be between the integers in the positions $(0, \frac{1}{2}n - 1)$ and $(0, \frac{1}{2}n)$, dividing the square into two equal halves. Every half-row in the square must then consist of sequences of $\frac{1}{2}n$ consecutive integers that form blocks of width $\frac{1}{2}n$ columns. Here the smallest corner block is $B_0(n_1, \frac{1}{2}n)$.

Suppose now that there is more than one gap > 1 in the top row, so that one of the gaps must occur within either the left or the right half of the row. Reverse similarity of rows ensures that each gap > 1 in the left half of the top row, read from left to right, must be matched by an equal gap > 1 in the right half, read from right to left – and vice versa.

Let the first gap > 1, read from left to right, occur between the position immediately before $(0, f_1)$, where f_1 can be taken as any integer $1 < f_1 < n$. Note that $f_1 \neq 1$, as the first two integers in the top row are always 0 1. This value, f_1, must be associated with an integer n_1, say, to form a smallest corner block $B_0(n_1, f_1)$ as has been shown in Section 4.2.

If $n_1 = 1$, the difference between the integers at $(0, f_1 - 1)$ and $(0, f_1)$ is 1. That is to say, there is no gap > 1 between the positions, contrary to the requirement that $B_0(n_1, f_1)$ is a corner block. Therefore $n_1 > 1$ and so $1 < n_1 \leq n$. Hence, the smallest possible smallest corner block occurs when $f_1 = 2, n_1 = 2$, namely the block $B_0(2,2)$.

4.4 Constructing successively larger corner blocks from smaller blocks

4.4.1 Blocks similar to $B_0(n_1, f_1)$

Consider the different ways in which blocks similar to the smallest corner block can be arranged to cover the square. BLOCKS SIMILAR TO THE SMALLEST CORNER BLOCK $B_0(n_1, f_1)$, are, by definition, blocks similar to the smallest corner block $B_0(n_1, f_1)$ (Section 4.1.3). They are completely specified by the integer in their top-left corner, namely,

$$0, \quad n_1 f_1, \quad 2n_1 f_1, \quad \ldots, \quad [(n^2/n_1 f_1) - 1]\, n_1 f_1.$$

Let $B_g(n_1, f_1)$ denote the block with the integer $g n_1 f_1$ in its top-left corner, where $0 \leq g < n^2/n_1 f_1$. Note that the blocks must be arranged so that the integers in their top-left corner, $g n_1 f_1$, also conform to the conditions of principal reversible squares, i.e.

(i) they must lie in n/n_1 rows and n/f_1 columns with integers arranged in ascending order, the top row starting with 0 1;

(ii) the rows and the columns thus formed must have reverse similarity and be similar and have equal cross sums.

4.4.2 Placing blocks similar to B_0 (n_1, f_1) along the top of the square

Consider first the different ways in which blocks similar to the corner block B_0 (n_1, f_1) can be arranged to fill the top n_1 rows of the square.

If $f_1 \neq n$, $(0, f_1)$ is the position immediately after the first gap > 1 in the top row. Then, as f_1 must be a factor of n, $2f_1 \leq n$ and so there must be a block adjacent and to the right of B_0 (n_1, f_1), entirely within the square. This new block, occupying the top n_1 partial rows of the next f_1 partial columns, must be the block with the integer $n_1 f_1$ in its top-left corner, i.e. the block B_1 (n_1, f_1) (Section 4.2.2). In block terms, this is because there is nowhere else for B_1 (n_1, f_1) to be placed if the square is to remain a principal reversible square. For, if B_1 (n_1, f_1) were to be placed immediately below B_0 (n_1, f_1), then the smallest corner block would no longer have n_1 rows but $2n_1$ rows, and then B_0 (n_1, f_1) would no longer be a smallest corner block. If B_1 (n_1, f_1) were to be placed anywhere else, then there would be blocks containing integers $> n_1 f_1$ that are either to the left of or above the integer $n_1 f_1$ in B_1 (n_1, f_1), again contrary to the conditions governing a principal reversible square. Hence, the gap immediately before the position $(0, f_1)$ that divides the corner block from its adjacent block, is of size $(n_1 f_1 - (f_1 - 1))$.

If $2f_1 < (n - f_1)$, a third similar block B_2 (n_1, f_1), with the integer $2n_1 f_1$ in its top-left corner and lying entirely within the square, can then be placed next to the block B_1 (n_1, f_1) along the top of the square. The gap in the top row that separates the second and third blocks is then of the same size, $n_1 f_1 - (f_1 - 1)$, as the gap that separates the corner block and the adjacent (second) block, B_1 (n_1, f_1). With each successive similar block so placed along the top of the square, provided that its top-left corner is still within the top row, the gaps > 1 in the top row that separate them remain the same.

4.4.3 Creating layers of blocks similar to B_0 (n_1, f_1) to form a new larger corner block B_0 (n_2, f_2)

Consider now what happens when one of these blocks similar to B_0 (n_1, f_1), say B_g (n_1, f_1), i.e. the block with the integer $gn_1 f_1$ $(1 < g)$ in its top-left corner, instead of being placed along the top of the square with its top-left corner at $(0, gf_1)$, is placed somewhere else. This can only be done if $gf_1 \leq \frac{1}{2}n$ and a factor of n, otherwise the placement process cannot be completed (Section 4.4.4). Because the integers in a principal reversible square are arranged in ascending order, the only other position to place

$B_g(n_1, f_1)$ is with its top-left corner at $(n_1, 0)$. This placement determines, by equal cross sums, a second layer of g blocks lying immediately beneath the g blocks already in place along the top of the square. Provided $2n_1$ is a factor of n, these two layers create a potential for a new larger corner block of depth $2n_1$ rows and width gf_1 columns, namely $B_0(2n_1, gf_1)$. The block $B_1(2n_1, gf_1)$ can then be placed with its top-left corner at $(0, gf_1)$ to form the new adjacent block.

Alternatively, this process can, in general, continue for several, say h, layers before, finally, the next block, namely $B_{gh}(n_1, f_1)$, is placed in the top layer. This LAYERING PROCESS can stop only at a layer for which hn_1 is a factor of n, as otherwise the further build-up of the square cannot be completed in this way.

After the layering process (when this is possible) is complete, a new larger corner block, $B_0(hn_1, gf_1)$, is created. Call this the corner block $B_0(n_2, f_2)$, where $n_2 = hn_1$, $f_2 = gf_1$. To preserve equal cross sums, the new corner block $B_0(n_2, f_2)$ must be replicated in the same manner as the original corner block $B_0(n_1, f_1)$. That is to say, g_2 blocks similar to $B_0(n_2, f_2)$ are placed along the top of the square (as $f_2 = gf_1 < \frac{1}{2}n$), and then, provided that $g_2 f_2 < \frac{1}{2}n$ and $n_2 < n$, in h_2 layers (where $h_2 n_2$ is a factor of n) of g_2 blocks similar to $B_0(n_2, f_2)$ down the square.

This BLOCK BUILDING PROCEDURE can be repeated with corner blocks of ever-increasing size $B_0(n_i, f_i)$, where f_i and n_i are factors of n, until either $f_i = n$ or $n_i = n$. The process must then stop, as then there is no space left for a larger corner block. Note that the blocks must be increasing in size in both rows **and** columns.

4.4.4 The largest corner block

This process of defining new and larger corner blocks can continue for as long as there are sufficient factors of n to define new positions $(0, f_1)$, $(0, f_2)$, ... , immediately before which new gaps of increasing sizes first occur, where

$$1 < f_1 < f_2 < f_3 < \ldots \le n$$

and each f_i is a factor of n and an integral multiple of all its predecessors. Each of these PROGRESSIVE FACTORS of n, namely $f_1, f_2, f_3, \ldots$, has to be paired, respectively, with an independent succession of progressive factors $n_1, n_2, n_3, \ldots$, of n that must satisfy the expression

$$1 < n_1 < n_2 < n_3 < \ldots \le n,$$

where again each n_i is a factor of n and an integral multiple of all its predecessors.[*]

---

[*] The method of using progressive factors was used by Rosser and Walker (1939, pp. 720–721) in constructing their normalized primitive squares, but neither proof nor enumeration was provided. Normalized primitive squares are equivalent to reversible squares.

5

Enumerating the different configurations of largest corner blocks

5.1 The objective

5.1.1 General statement

In every principal reversible square there is a largest corner block. In Chapter 4 a method of constructing configurations of this largest corner block was given. The requirement now is to enumerate these different configurations of the largest corner block, $B_0(n, f)$, where f is a factor of n such that $1 < f \leq n$.

A largest corner block has been shown to be completely defined by the positions and sizes of the first occurrences, read from left to right, of gaps > 1 of increasing sizes in its top row (Section 4.4.4). These gaps > 1 (if any) of increasing size occur immediately before the positions $(0, f_1)$, $(0, f_2)$, ... , $(0, f)$, where $f_1, f_2, \dots , f$ are progressive factors of f that satisfy (4.4.4.1), namely

$$1 < f_1 < f_2 < \dots < f \leq n,$$

i.e. each factor is an integral multiple of all lesser factors. The integers in these positions have been shown to be, respectively, $n_1 f_1, n_2 f_2, \dots , nf$, where $n_1, n_2, \dots$ are progressive factors of n that satisfy (4.4.4.2), namely

$$1 < n_1 < n_2 < \dots \leq n.$$

By definition, the gap > 1 immediately before the position $(0, f)$ is the first occurrence of the largest size of gap in the top row of the square. The requirement is to enumerate the different configurations of largest corner blocks $B_0(n, f)$ of width f columns and depth n partial rows.

There will be a variety of different ways of selecting a number, say v, of progressive factors of f for the factors $f_1, f_2, \dots$. These are paired respectively with selections of v progressive factors of n. The blocks $B_0(n_1, f_1)$, $B_0(n_2, f_2)$, ... , $B_0(n_v, f_v)$ then define the corner blocks wholly contained within the largest corner block $B_0(n, f)$. Blocks similar to any one of these corner blocks can be arranged to cover exactly the next larger corner block, by using the block-building procedure described in Section 4.4.3. In particular, blocks similar to $B_0(n_v, f_v)$ will cover exactly the largest corner block $B_0(n, f)$.

There is one and only one possibility of having no gap > 1 in the top row of the largest corner block and thus of there being no intervening factors > 1. (If, then, there is a first gap > 1 in the top row of the completed square, it will be immediately before the position $(0, f)$.) The requirement, now, is to enumerate the additional number of different ways (if any) of selecting factors of f to give

> (i) gaps > 1 of one and only one size within the top row of the largest corner block, the first occurrences of a gap of this size being immediately before $(0, f_1)$, with $1 < f_1 < f$;
>
> (ii) gaps > 1 of two and only two different sizes, the first occurrences of which are immediately before $(0, f_1)$ and $(0, f_2)$ respectively, with $1 < f_1 < f_2 < f$;

and so on.

In general, the requirement is to find, first, the number of different ways (if any) of there being gaps > 1 of, say, v different sizes within the top row of the largest corner block, where v is any non-negative integer as yet unspecified, the first occurrences of which are immediately before $(0, f_1)$, $(0, f_2)$, ... , $(0, f_v)$, respectively, with $1 < f_1 < f_2 < ... < f_v < f$. The selected v progressive factors $f_1, f_2, ... , f_v$ of f then have to be paired with any selection of v progressive factors $n_1, n_2, ... , n_v$ of n, with $1 < n_1 < n_2 < ... < n_v < n$. The pairings then define corner blocks $B_0(n_i, f_i)$, $1 \le i \le v$, and thus determine the sizes of the gaps > 1 immediately before the positions $(0, f_i)$. Each different selection of v progressive factors of f, when paired in turn with each available selection of v progressive factors of n, gives a different configuration for the largest corner block. When all possible different selections and pairings have been identified and enumerated, the resulting summation of these possibilities gives the required total of different configurations for the largest corner block $B_0(n, f)$, for any particular value of f.

5.1.2 Strategy

Let $F_n(f)$ denote the number of possible different configurations of the largest corner block, $B_0(n, f)$. To enumerate these configurations, it is convenient to restrict the possible values of n not only to be doubly even but, in the first instance, also to having only one other prime, say p:

$$n = 2^r p^s \quad r, s \text{ integers such that } r > 1, s \ge 0. \qquad (5.1.2.1)$$

Then f must also be the product of powers of 2 and/or p:

$$f = 2^{r'}p^{s'} \leq n \quad r', s' \text{ integers such that } 0 \leq r' \leq r,$$
$$0 \leq s' \leq s, 0 < (r' + s'); \qquad (5.1.2.2)$$

Let t' be the maximum number of progressive factors of f with 1 and f excluded. Starting at 1, the next progressive factor of f can be obtained by increasing by 1 each time either the power of 2 or the power of p, until both $2^{r'}$ and $p^{s'}$ are reached, so

$$t' = r' + s' - 1. \qquad (5.1.2.3)$$

Let t be the maximum number of progressive factors of n with 1 and n excluded, so

$$t = r + s - 1. \qquad (5.1.2.4)$$

As $t' \leq t$, the number of progressive factors chosen, v, must be such that $0 \leq v \leq t'$.

To calculate $F_n(f)$, first repeat the following three steps for all values of v:

(i) find the number of ways, say $W_v(f)$, in which v progressive factors of $f = 2^{r'}p^{s'}$ can be chosen, in terms of r', s';

(ii) find the number of ways, say $W_v(n)$, in which v progressive factors of $n = 2^r p^s$ can be chosen, in terms of r, s;

(iii) multiply $W_v(f)$ and $W_v(n)$ to get the number of different configurations of a corner block $B_0(n, f)$ having v progressive factors.

Then sum the products $W_v(f) W_v(n)$, over all values of v from 0 to t' to give, in general,

$$F_n(f) = \sum_{0 \leq v \leq t'} W_v(f) W_v(n) \quad f = 2^{r'}p^{s'}, \quad 1 < f \leq n. \qquad (5.1.2.5)$$

5.2 The number of ways of choosing v progressive factors of f and of n

Exactly the same method can be used to determine the number of ways of choosing v progressive factors of f and of n, i.e. such that each factor is a multiple of all lesser factors. The logic of the method requires, first, the consideration of 'paths' through 'tables of factors'.

Arrange the factors of n, $2^j p^i$, $0 \leq j < r$, $0 \leq i < s$, in an array in the manner shown in Table 5.2, i.e. in such a way that the entry in the position row i, column j is $2^j p^i$. Call this array the FACTOR TABLE of n, or the n-factor table.

5.2.1 Progressive paths through the table of factors of f

The f-factor table is a sub-array of the n-factor table, Table 5.2, consisting of

Table 5.2 Factor table of $n = 2^r p^s$

1	2	4	...	$2^{r'}$	...	2^r
p^1	$2p^1$	$4p^1$	...	$2^{r'}p^1$	...	$2^r p^1$
p^2	$2p^2$	$4p^2$	...	$2^{r'}p^2$	...	$2^r p^2$
$\vdots$	$\vdots$	$\vdots$	$\vdots$	$\vdots$	$\vdots$	$\vdots$
$p^{s'}$	$2p^{s'}$	$4p^{s'}$	...	$2^{r'}p^{s'}$	...	$2^r p^{s'}$
$\vdots$	$\vdots$	$\vdots$	$\vdots$	$\vdots$	$\vdots$	$\vdots$
p^s	$2p^s$	$4p^s$	...	$2^{r'}p^s$	...	$2^r p^s$

the leftmost $r' + 1$ partial columns and top $s' + 1$ partial rows. It is required to find in how many different ways v progressive factors can be selected from this f-factor table.

Consider any particular factor in the table, say, for example, $2^{r^*}p^{s^*}$. Then the only factors of $2^{r^*}p^{s^*}$ are the factors $2^{r^*-}p^{s^*-}$, say, where $0 \le r^{*-} \le r^*$, $0 \le s^{*-} \le s^*$; and the only factors within the table that are integral multiples of $2^{r^*}p^{s^*}$ are the factors $2^{r^{*+}}p^{s^{*+}}$, where $r^* \le r^{*+} \le r'$, $s^* \le s^{*+} \le s'$.

Define a PROGRESSIVE PATH in an x-factor table as any unbroken sequence of factors that progresses through the table starting at 1, then moving from one factor to the next, either from left to right in the same row, or vertically downward in the same column, and ending at the factor x. In other words, starting at $2^0 p^0$ and then moving from $2^{r^*}p^{s^*}$ to either $2^{r^*+1}p^{s^*}$ or $2^{r^*}p^{s^*+1}$, until x has been reached.

The only ways in which progressive factors can be selected from the f-factor table is when the successive factors are elements within a progressive path in the f-factor table. As each progressive path in the f-factor table has to move r' columns to the right and s' rows down to reach f, the number of factors in a progressive path, with 1 and f excluded, is $(r' + s' - 1) = t'$.

A pictorial representation of the 35 progressive paths for $f = 2^4 p^3$ is shown in Figure 5.2.1. If, for example, with $f = 2^4 p^3$, rows 0 and 2 and columns 1 and 3 were chosen, then the progressive path is as shown in Table 5.2.1.

Table 5.2.1 A progressive path through the table of factors for $f = 2^4 p^3$

1 $\rightarrow$	2	2^2	2^3	2^4
	$\downarrow$			
p	$2p$	$2^2 p$	$2^3 p$	$2^4 p$
	$\downarrow$			
p^2	$2p^2 \rightarrow$	$2^2 p^2 \rightarrow$	$2^3 p^2$	$2^4 p^2$
			$\downarrow$	
p^3	$2p^3$	$2^2 p^3$	$2^3 p^3 \rightarrow$	$2^4 p^3$

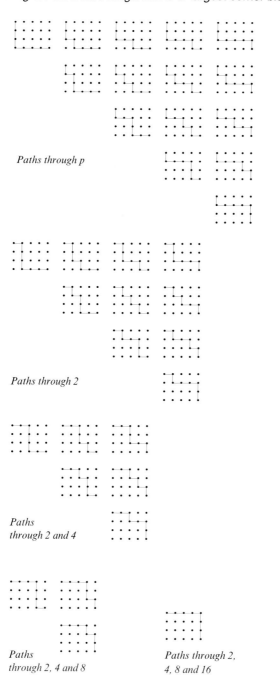

Paths through p

Paths through 2

Paths through 2 and 4

Paths through 2, 4 and 8

Paths through 2, 4, 8 and 16

Figure 5.2.1 Progressive paths through the factor table for $2^4 p^3$.

5.2.2 Steps that select a progressive path

As explained above, any v progressive factors within the table of factors of f must lie along a progressive path, a characteristic of which is that the route from the top-left corner to the bottom-right corner is always either to the right or downward. Call each change of direction from moving horizontally to the right to moving vertically downward, i.e. from $2^{r^*}p^{s^*}$ to $2^{r^*}p^{s^*+1}$, a STEP. For example, in Table 5.2.2 there are two steps, at 2 and 2^3p^2.

A completed progressive path has to move r' positions to the right and s' positions downward, the moves taking place in any combination. By definition, steps always occur in different rows and in different columns. Hence **the total number of ways of choosing, say, i steps is the number of ways of choosing i integers from r' integers multiplied by the number of ways of choosing i integers from s' integers**. That is to say the number of ways of choosing paths with i steps is $\binom{r'}{i}\binom{s'}{i}$.

It is easily verified in Figure 5.2.1 that, in the 35 progressive paths of 2^4p^2, there are:

$$\binom{4}{0}\binom{3}{0} = 1 \text{ path with no step;}$$

$$\binom{4}{1}\binom{3}{1} = 12 \text{ paths with 1 step;}$$

$$\binom{4}{2}\binom{3}{2} = 18 \text{ paths with 2 steps and}$$

$$\binom{4}{3}\binom{3}{3} = 4 \text{ paths with 3 steps.}$$

5.2.3 The number of ways, $W_v(f)$, of choosing v factors from within the progressive paths of the f-factor table

Consider now the number of ways of choosing v factors from a progressive path. Each progressive path contains $t' = (r' + s' - 1)$ factors (when 1 and f are excluded) and there are $\binom{r'}{i}\binom{s'}{i}$ different paths that contain i steps. Remember that for factors of f to satisfy (4.4.4.1) not all the t' factors have to be present.

$W_v(f)$ denotes the number of different ways in which just v progressive factors of f can be selected. Suppose that i of these v factors define steps, so that $(v - i)$ do not define steps. There are $\binom{r'}{i}\binom{s'}{i}$ possible ways of choosing those i progressive factors that select the steps that define a progressive path. From the remaining $(t' - i)$ progressive factors in a path selected by the i steps, $(v - i)$ are needed to make up the total of v factors. There are $\binom{t'-i}{v-i}$ ways of choosing them from the remaining $(t' - i)$ progressive factors.

It follows that the total number of different ways of choosing a total of v progressive factors (i of which define the positions of steps, and $(v - i)$ of which do not define steps) is given by the expression

$$W_v(f) = \sum_{0 \le i \le v} \binom{r'}{i}\binom{s'}{i}\binom{t'-i}{v-i}, \quad 0 \le v \le t' = r' + s' - 1.$$

It is useful, for Section 5.3.4, to generalize this formula to include the terms outside the ranges specified for both i and v, although this has no correlate in a factor table. Note that, if $i < 0$, then both the first two binomial coefficients are zero by definition (Appendix A.1). Also, if $v < i$, then the third binomial coefficient is zero. So the summation can be taken over all values of i.

Consider the different possible values of v outside the range 0 to t'. If $v < 0$, then:

- for $v < i$ the third binomial coefficient is zero, and
- for $i \leq v, i < 0$ and so the first two binomial coefficients are zero;

hence, for $v < 0$, their product is zero. If $t' < v$, then:

- for $i \leq t', 0 \leq (t' - i) < (v - i)$ and the third binomial coefficient is zero, and
- for $t' < i$ the first two binomial coefficients are zero;[*]

so for $t' < v$ the product is zero as well. Hence for v outside the range of 0 to t', all the terms are zero and the restriction of $0 \leq v \leq t'$ can be dropped as well, to give

$$W_v(f) = \begin{cases} \sum_i \binom{r'}{i}\binom{s'}{i}\binom{t' - i}{v - i} & f = 2^{r'}p^{s'}, 0 \leq t' = (r' + s' - 1); \\ 0 & \text{otherwise.} \end{cases} \quad (5.2.3.1)$$

Numerical values for $W_v(f)$ for $0 \leq r' \leq 5$ and $0 \leq s' \leq 4$ are shown in Table 5.2.3.

5.2.4 The value of $W_v(n)$

The arguments that lead to the formula (5.2.3.1) for $f = 2^r p^{s'}$ can equally apply to n.

$W_v(n)$ denotes the number of different ways of choosing v factors of n along progressive paths through the n-factor table, Table 5.2. The length of each progressive path, with 1 and n excluded, is $(r + s - 1)$. Then, from (5.2.3.1),

$$W_v(n) = \begin{cases} \sum_j \binom{r}{j}\binom{s}{j}\binom{t - j}{v - j} & n = 2^r p^s, t = (r + s - 1); \\ 0 & \text{otherwise.} \end{cases} \quad (5.2.4.1)$$

---

[*] Since their upper index is positive but less than their lower index; see note to (I.1) in Appendix A.2.2.

Table 5.2.3 $W_v(f)$ for small values of $f = 2^{r'}p^{s'}$

	$W_0(f)$	$W_1(f)$	$W_2(f)$	$W_3(f)$	$W_4(f)$	$W_5(f)$	$W_6(f)$	$W_7(f)$	$W_8(f)$	...
$s' = 0, r' = 1$	1									
$r' = 2$	1	1								
$r' = 3$	1	2	1							
$r' = 4$	1	3	3	1						
$r' = 5$	1	4	6	4	1					
$\vdots$	$\vdots$	$\vdots$	$\vdots$	$\vdots$	$\vdots$	$\vdots$	$\vdots$			
$s' = 1, r' = 0$	1									
$r' = 1$	1	2								
$r' = 2$	1	4	3							
$r' = 3$	1	6	9	4						
$r' = 4$	1	8	18	16	5					
$r' = 5$	1	10	30	40	25	6				
$\vdots$	$\vdots$	$\vdots$	$\vdots$	$\vdots$	$\vdots$	$\vdots$	$\vdots$	$\vdots$		
$s' = 2, r' = 0$	1	1								
$r' = 1$	1	4	3							
$r' = 2$	1	7	12	6						
$r' = 3$	1	10	27	28	10					
$r' = 4$	1	13	48	76	55	15				
$r' = 5$	1	16	75	160	175	96	21			
$\vdots$	$\vdots$	$\vdots$	$\vdots$	$\vdots$	$\vdots$	$\vdots$	$\vdots$	$\vdots$	$\vdots$	
$s' = 3, r' = 0$	1	2	1							
$r' = 1$	1	6	9	4						
$r' = 2$	1	10	27	28	10					
$r' = 3$	1	14	55	92	70	20				
$r' = 4$	1	18	93	216	255	150	35			
$r' = 5$	1	22	141	420	675	606	287	56		
$\vdots$	$\vdots$	$\vdots$	$\vdots$	$\vdots$	$\vdots$	$\vdots$	$\vdots$	$\vdots$	$\vdots$	$\vdots$
$s' = 4, r' = 0$	1	3	3	1						
$r' = 1$	1	8	18	16	5					
$r' = 2$	1	13	48	76	55	15				
$r' = 3$	1	18	93	216	255	150	35			
$r' = 4$	1	23	153	471	780	720	350	70		
$r' = 5$	1	28	228	876	1875	2376	1778	728	126	
$\vdots$	$\vdots$	$\vdots$	$\vdots$	$\vdots$	$\vdots$	$\vdots$	$\vdots$	$\vdots$	$\vdots$	$\vdots$

...

Note: The table is also valid for $n = 2^r p^s$, $r > 1$, if n, r and s are used in place of f, r' and s' respectively, provided that the values $r = 0$ and $r = 1$ are ignored.

Table 7.2.3 The triples of non-decreasing factors of $n = 2^2 \times 3 \times 5$

Third factor — Exponent of (2 / 3 / 5), columns shown as combined codes:

Exponent of:	2:	0	0	0	0	1	1	1	1	2	2	2	2
	3:	0	0	1	1	0	0	1	1	0	0	1	1
235: 235:	5:	0	1	0	1	0	1	0	1	0	1	0	1

First and second factors, with Number of: −, =, ≡, *

First and second factors	000	001	010	011	100	101	110	111	200	201	210	211	−	=	≡	*
000 000	≡	≡	=	=	=	=	=	=	=	=	=	=		10	2	
000 001	.	=	.	−	.	−	.	−	.	.	−	=	4	2		
000 010	.	.	=	−	.	.	−	−	.	.	−	=	4	2		
000 011	.	.	.	=	.	.	.	−	.	.	.	=	1	2		
000 100	.	.	.	.	=	−	−	−	−	−	−	=	6	2		
000 101	.	.	.	.	.	=	.	−	.	−	.	=	2	2		
000 110	.	.	.	.	.	.	=	−	.	.	−	=	2	2		
000 111	.	.	.	.	.	.	.	=	.	.	.	=		2		
000 200	.	.	.	.	.	.	.	.	=	−	−	=	2	2		
000 201	.	.	.	.	.	.	.	.	.	=	.	=		2		
000 210	.	.	.	.	.	.	.	.	.	.	=	=		2		
000 211	.	.	.	.	.	.	.	.	.	.	.	≡			1	
001 001	.	=	.	−	.	−	.	−	.	−	.	=	4	2		
001 011	.	.	.	−	.	.	.	*	.	.	.	−	2			1
001 101	.	.	.	−	.	.	.	*	.	*	.	−	2			2
001 111	.	.	.	−	.	.	.	.	.	.	.	−	2			
001 201	.	.	.	.	.	.	.	−	.	.	.	−	2			
001 211	.	.	.	.	.	.	.	.	.	.	.	=		1		
010 010	.	.	=	−	.	.	−	−	.	.	−	=	4	2		
010 011	.	.	.	−	.	.	.	*	.	.	.	−	2			1
010 110	.	.	.	.	.	−	.	*	.	*	.	−	2			2
010 111	.	.	.	−	.	.	.	.	.	.	.	−	2			
010 210	.	.	.	.	.	.	.	−	.	.	.	−	2			
010 211	.	.	.	.	.	.	.	.	.	.	.	=		1		
011 011	.	.	.	=	.	.	.	−	.	.	.	=	1	2		
011 111	.	.	.	−	.	.	.	.	.	.	.	−	2			
011 211	.	.	.	.	.	.	.	.	.	.	.	=		1		
100 100	.	.	.	.	=	−	−	−	−	−	−	=	6	2		
100 101	.	.	.	.	.	−	.	*	.	*	.	−	2			2
100 110	.	.	.	.	.	.	−	*	.	*	.	−	2			2
100 111	.	.	.	.	.	.	.	−	.	.	.	−	2			
100 200	.	.	.	.	.	.	.	.	−	*	*	−	2			2
100 201	.	.	.	.	.	.	.	.	.	−	.	−	2			
100 210	.	.	.	.	.	.	.	.	.	.	−	−	2			
100 211	.	.	.	.	.	.	.	.	.	.	.	=		1		
101 101	.	.	.	.	.	=	.	−	.	−	.	=	2	2		
101 111	.	.	.	.	.	.	.	−	.	.	.	−	2			
101 201	.	.	.	.	.	.	.	.	.	−	.	−	2			
101 211	.	.	.	.	.	.	.	.	.	.	.	=		1		
110 110	.	.	.	.	.	.	=	−	.	.	−	=	2	2		
110 111	.	.	.	.	.	.	.	−	.	.	.	−	2			
110 210	.	.	.	.	.	.	.	.	.	.	−	−	2			
110 211	.	.	.	.	.	.	.	.	.	.	.	=		1		
111 111	.	.	.	.	.	.	.	=	.	.	.	=		2		
111 211	.	.	.	.	.	.	.	.	.	.	.	=		1		
200 200	.	.	.	.	.	.	.	.	=	−	−	=	2	2		
200 201	.	.	.	.	.	.	.	.	.	−	.	−	2			
200 210	.	.	.	.	.	.	.	.	.	.	−	−	2			
200 211	.	.	.	.	.	.	.	.	.	.	.	=		1		
201 201	.	.	.	.	.	.	.	.	.	=	.	=		2		
201 211	.	.	.	.	.	.	.	.	.	.	.	=		1		
210 210	.	.	.	.	.	.	.	.	.	.	=	=		2		
210 211	.	.	.	.	.	.	.	.	.	.	.	=		1		
211 211	.	.	.	.	.	.	.	.	.	.	.	≡			1	
Totals:													84	60	4	12

$$84 + 60 + 4 + 12 = 160$$

(vii) If slot S_v is empty, fill it with factor n.

(viii) Fill any empty slot with the factor in the slot to its right, until all the slots are full.

(ix) Remove slot S_0 to give a sequence of v factors.

Any of the $(v + 1)$ slots can be the empty slot. So there are $(v + 1) = \binom{v+1}{v}$ possibilities for each selection of the $(v - 1)$ factors that have been chosen at step (i). The result of this procedure is:

after step: (vi)   (ix)
$$[-, 1, f_1, f_2, \ \ldots\ , f_{v-1}]$$ $$[1, f_1, f_2, \ \ldots\ , f_{v-1}];$$
$$[1, -, f_1, f_2, \ \ldots\ , f_{v-1}]$$ $$[f_1, f_1, f_2, \ \ldots\ , f_{v-1}];$$
$$[1, f_1, -, f_2, \ \ldots\ , f_{v-1}]$$ $$[f_1, f_2, f_2, \ \ldots\ , f_{v-1}];$$
$$\vdots$$ $$\vdots$$
$$[1, f_1, f_2, \ \ldots\ , -, f_{v-1}]$$ $$[f_1, f_2, f_3, \ \ldots\ , f_{v-1}, f_{v-1}];$$
$$[1, f_1, f_2, \ \ldots\ , f_{v-1}, -]$$ $$[f_1, f_2, f_3, \ \ldots\ , f_{v-1}, n].$$

As the total number of sequences of $(v - 1)$-tuples of factors is $\prod_g \binom{s_g + v - 1}{v - 1}$, the number of sequences that will be excluded at this stage is $\binom{v+1}{v} \prod_g \binom{s_g + v - 1}{v - 1}$.

However, some sequences have been counted more than once, for example if $f_1 = f_2$, then the second and third of the sequences above are identical. To avoid this multiple counting, add back in all sequences in which **more than one** of the three conditions (commence with the factor 1, end with the factor n or have a copy of any factor) holds, using the above steps (i) to (ix) but adapted to select $(v - 1)$ factors for $(v + 1)$ slots. This will give $\binom{v+1}{v-1} \prod_g \binom{s_g + v - 2}{v - 2}$ sequences that must be added back.

Again this process will count some sequences more than once, and these multiple countings can be excluded by using steps (i) to (ix) for selecting $(v - 2)$ of the $(v + 1)$ slots for placing $(v - 2)$ factors, and so on. At the final step one of the $(v + 1)$ slots is selected (in $\binom{v+1}{1}$ ways) and filled with the factor 1 and then the steps (vii) to (ix) are used to build a sequence of v factors that will all be 1's and n's.

The general version of steps (i) to (ix) is:

(i) Consider each possible sequence of non-decreasing i-tuples of factors in turn, for example the i-tuple $(f_1, f_2, f_3, \ \ldots\ , f_i)$.

(ii) Append to the beginning of the i-tuple the factor 1, for example $(1, f_1, f_2, f_3, \ \ldots\ , f_i)$.

(iii) Consider $(v + 1)$ slots labelled $S_0, S_1, S_2, \ldots, S_v$.

(iv) Select $(i + 1)$ of them.

(v) Order the selected slots into ascending order of their subscript.

(vi) Place the $(i + 1)$ factors from step (ii) into these slots, in ascending order.

(vii) If slot S_v is empty, fill it with factor n.

(viii) Fill any remaining empty slot with the factor in the slot to its right, until all the slots are full.

(ix) Remove slot S_0 to give a sequence of i factors.

This process will give v-tuples of factors in which one of the three conditions (1 as a factor, n as a factor, a pair of factors identical), holds at least $(v - i)$ times, since:

- if the factor 1 was placed in slot S_0 at step (vi), and so removed at step (ix), there were $(v - i)$ empty slots that were filled, at steps (vii) and (viii), with copies of either one of the original factors, $f_1, f_2, f_3, \ldots, f_i$, or of n;
- if the factor 1 was not placed in slot S_0 at step (vi), it is placed there at step (viii) but S_0 was removed at the next step. The remaining $(v - i - 1)$ empty slots were filled, at steps (vii) and (viii), with copies of either one of the original factors, $f_1, f_2, f_3, \ldots, f_i$, or n. These, together with the factor 1 inserted at step (vi) and still present, ensure that there are at least $(v - i)$ 1's, n's or copies of the original factors in the v-tuple of factors.

If the factors $f_1, f_2, f_3, \ldots, f_i$ are all unique and do not include 1 or n, then there will be no double counting and the number of sequences created at step (iv) will be $\binom{v+1}{i+1}$. But if $f_1, f_2, f_3, \ldots, f_i$ are not unique or do include 1 or n, then there will be double counting. So at the next stages all sequences with more than $(v - i)$ 1's, n's or copies must be added back.

This process is repeated for $(v - 1) \geq i \geq 0$, to give the general form of the equation (7.1.6), repeated here:

$$W_v(n) = \sum_i (-1)^{v+i} \binom{v+1}{i+1} \prod_g \binom{s_g + i}{i}, \qquad 0 \leq v < \sum_g s_g.$$

As a check, note that there are no sequences of four progressive factors when $n = 60$ and that, indeed, (7.1.6) gives $W_4(60) = 0$.

7.3 Enumeration for small values of n

Substituting the values of $W_v(n)$ and $W_{v+1}(n)$ into (7.1.5) and summing over v will give the value of N_n. The actual values of N_n for n up to $2^4 p_1^3 p_2^2 p_3$ are given in Table 7.3. The value of M_n, the number of essentially different reversible squares that can be reached by legitimate transformations of a principal reversible square, is unaltered from that given for $n = 2^r p^s$, being $2^{n-2}\{(\tfrac{1}{2}n)!\}^2$ (2.4.2.1). The total number of essentially different reversible squares, and so of essentially different most-perfect squares (Section 3.3), is the product $N_n M_n$.

Table 7.3 Enumeration of principal reversible squares
of order $n = \prod_g p_g^{s_g}$ up to $2^4 p_1^3 p_2^2 p_3$

$s_1\,s_2\,s_3$	$s_0 = 2$	$s_0 = 3$	$s_0 = 4$
0 0 0	3	10	35
1 0 0	42	230	1,190
1 1 0	1,158	9,350	66,290
1 1 1	52,422	583,670	5,404,490
1 2 0	16,782	180,990	1,636,740
1 2 1	1,083,318	15,509,070	178,011,540
2 0 0	393	3,030	20,790
2 1 0	16,782	180,990	1,636,740
2 1 1	1,083,318	15,509,070	178,011,540
2 2 0	334,833	4,676,670	52,682,490
2 2 1	29,438,142	528,903,630	7,384,720,140
3 0 0	3,030	30,670	264,740
3 1 0	180,990	2,474,030	27,413,540
3 1 1	15,509,070	274,043,390	3,776,451,140
3 2 0	4,676,670	80,988,270	1,098,857,340
3 2 1	528,903,630	11,521,530,270	190,441,098,540

7.4 Summary

If the formulae for the $W_v(n)$ and the $W_{v+1}(n)$, the number of ways of selecting v progressive factors of any doubly-even n, as given by (7.1.6), are substituted into (7.1.5), the result is an expression for N_n, the number of principal reversible squares. This expression has three summations, over v and, say, i and j. The number of binomial coefficients that include just i, or just j, is equal to the number of prime factors in n. So it is not possible to find a closed-form solution that eliminates i and j. It can be shown that the binomial coefficients in which v occurs can be reduced to just two, to give the summation $\sum_v \binom{v+1}{i+1}\binom{v+1}{j}$. However, there is no closed-form solution to this summation.[*] So there is no closed-form solution to the expression for N_n.

Consequently, to obtain the number of principal reversible squares, N_n, the values of $W_v(n)$ and $W_{v+1}(n)$ are first computed from (7.1.6) and then substituted into (7.1.5).

---

[*] The Zeilberger algorithm (Petkovšek *et al.*, 1996) fails to find a recurrence relationship.

8

Conclusion

8.1 On methods of construction

Before summarizing, we consider whether most-perfect squares could have been constructed and enumerated by any of the other known methods for constructing pandiagonal squares.

The method of constructing most-perfect squares via reversible squares, a sub-class of Rosser and Walker's (1939) primitive squares, was chosen in preference to other previously known methods for constructing pandiagonal squares (Section 1.5). The choice was based on an inspection of all the 8 by 8 most-perfect squares (Ollerenshaw, 1986), the most complete set of most-perfect squares previously available. Now that all most-perfect squares can be constructed, consider whether the alternative methods could be used for their construction.

To do this, we first need to establish a property of most-perfect squares that can help in deciding whether or not any particular method can generate all these squares. Consider a principal reversible square. The first gap > 1 in its top row, if any, is either immediately before the position $(0,2)$, i.e. $f_1 = 2$, or to the right of $(0,2)$, i.e. $f_1 > 2$. If there is no gap > 1 or if $f_1 > 2$, the integer at the position $(0,2)$ is 2. As $(0,2)$ is in an even row and column and, when $n > 4$, in the top left half of the square, 2 remains in this position when the reversible square is transformed into a most-perfect square by using (3.1.1.5). A most-perfect square can always be viewed as being made up of the sum of a radix and a unit auxiliary square, $P = nA + A'$ (Section 1.2). There is then a 0 at the position $(0,2)$ in the radix auxiliary A. It follows that there are then at least two 0's in the top row of the radix auxiliary. If, in contrast, $f_1 = 2$, then the integer at $(0,2)$ is $2n_1$, i.e. it depends on the depth of the smallest corner block $B_0(n_1, f_1)$. For $n_1 < \frac{1}{2}n$ the integer at $(0,2)$ is still less than n, so there is still a 0 at this position in the radix auxiliary square.

The only other possible values of n_1 are $\frac{1}{2}n$ and n. The integer at (0,2) would then be either n or $2n$, respectively. In both cases the unit auxiliary square A' has a 0 at (0,2), as well as at (0,0). Consequently, for $n > 4$ there are at least two occurrences of the integer 0 in the top row of either the radix or the unit auxiliary square of every most-perfect square that is a transform from a principal reversible square. This result is extended to all most-perfect squares in Appendix B.5.

8.2 Construction by using Latin auxiliary squares

For any $n > 4$ no most-perfect square that is a transform of a principal reversible square can be constructed directly from a pair of Latin auxiliary squares. This is because, by definition, a Latin square cannot have more than one copy of any integer in any row or any column and, as is shown in Appendix B.5, either the unit or the radix auxiliary of every most-perfect square ($n > 4$) must have at least two occurrences of 0 in one of its rows.

8.3 Construction by using paths

In the method of paths (Section 1.3.2) (Frost, 1878), if there are two or more copies of one integer in the same row (column) of an auxiliary square, there cannot be more than one occurrence of that integer in any of the columns (rows) of that same auxiliary square. In particular, as there are at least two copies of the integer 0 in one of the rows of either the unit or radix auxiliary square, there cannot be another copy of 0 in a column of the same auxiliary.

If $f_1 > 2$, there are at least two copies of 0 in the top row of the radix auxiliary square of the principal reversible square (Section 8.1). As when $n > 4$, the integer at the position (2,0) also remains fixed in the transformation, the integer at (2,0) in the reversible square must then also be $\geq n$ to avoid two occurrences of 0 in the left column of the radix square, as well as in the two copies of 0 in the top row. This rules out any smallest corner block except the blocks $B_0(2, \frac{1}{2}n)$ and $B_0(n, n)$. But there are always other smallest corner blocks that can be used in the construction for any $n > 4$, e.g. the block $B_0(4, 2)$. Hence, there are always, for any $n > 4$, most-perfect squares that cannot be constructed by the method of paths.

8.4 Construction by using the chess knight's path and mixed auxiliary squares

With the method of mixed auxiliary squares (Section 1.3.4) (Bellew, 1997), there can only be one copy of any integer, except 0, in the auxiliary squares combined. Hence, 2 cannot be the result of adding 1 from one auxiliary square and 1 from the other (1 + 1) but must arise from 2 + 0. When the integer 2 is at the position (0,2), as it always can be in a most-perfect square (Section 8.1), there must be a 0 at this same position in one of the auxiliary squares. But this is impossible, as there is no way for a chess knight's path to go from the position (0,0), where the integer 0 must be, to the position (0,2) when $n > 4$. It is therefore not possible to construct all the most-perfect squares for any $n > 4$ by using the method of mixed auxiliary squares.

8.5 In conclusion

Until now, methods for constructing magic squares have only been able to produce some of the members of the class of magic square for which they were designed (Section 1.3). Rosser and Walker (1939) were able to construct and enumerate all pandiagonal squares, but only for $n \leq 5$. Bellew (1997) enumerated pandiagonal squares, but only those constructed by using his method of mixed auxiliary squares. Bellew gave a general formula, but only for n not divisible by 2 (or 3), and so for none of the most-perfect squares. Moreover, for doubly-even $n > 4$, only some, not all, of the pandiagonal squares, in particular not all of the most-perfect squares, can be constructed by using the method of mixed auxiliary squares (Section 8.4).

Although the inventor of most-perfect pandiagonal squares, McClintock (1897), showed that his 'McClintock' squares have a one-to-one correspondence with most-perfect squares, his method for their construction was incomplete, and so he was unable to attempt an enumeration. Ollerenshaw (1989) claimed a method for construction of all most-perfect squares, based on McClintock squares, but only gave the enumeration for orders that were simple powers of 2 ($n = 2^r, r > 1$). Although it is possible to construct all McClintock squares by using an extension of McClintock's own method, for all doubly-even n, this extension is not simple to execute; nor is there a proof of its completeness. Previously, the only known method of construction that can produce all most-perfect squares was that of primitive squares (Rosser and Walker, 1939), but this method also produces pandiagonal squares that are not most-perfect. It is the method of primitive squares that has been restricted here to produce only most-perfect squares.

8.6 Summary

Our method of **construction**, based on the one-to-one correspondence of reversible and most-perfect squares, is well-defined and simple; it produces **all** most-perfect pandiagonal magic squares and no others (Chapter 4).

Our formula for **enumeration** of the number of principal reversible squares is

$$N_n = \sum_v W_v(n)\{W_v(n) + W_{v+1}(n)\}, \qquad \text{from (6.1.2)},$$

which is complete. No other known method has proved capable of enumerating all most-perfect squares.

The formula (6.1.2) merely sums products of the numbers of ways, $W_v(n)$, of selecting v progressive factors of n over all values of v. For $n = 2^r$ $(r > 1)$ the result of the substitution is

$$N_{2^r} = \binom{2r-1}{r}, \qquad \text{from (6.6.1)},$$

confirming the claim of Ollerenshaw (1989) (Section 1.4). For $N = 2^r p^s$ (p any prime $> 2, r > 1, s \geq 0$),

$$N_{2^r p^s} = \frac{1}{2}\binom{2s}{s}\sum_i \binom{s}{i}\binom{r+s}{r-i}\binom{2r+s-i}{r+s}, \qquad \text{from (6.5.4)},$$

a new result, with one index of summation that is irreducible to a closed form. In general, for all doubly-even n,

$$n = \prod_g p_g^{s_g} \qquad (p \text{ any prime}, p_0 = 2;\ g,\ s_g \text{ any positive integer}, s_0 > 1),$$

the number of ways of selecting v progressive factors is

$$W_v(n) = \sum_i (-1)^{v+i}\binom{v+1}{i+1}\prod_g\binom{s_g+i}{i}, \qquad \text{from (7.1.6)}.$$

These values of $W_v(n)$ and $W_{v+1}(n)$, when substituted into (6.1.2), give a formula for the value of N_n having three indices of summation. All of these summations are computable as their ranges for non-zero terms are bounded.

As the number of prime factors in n increases, the value of N_n increases rapidly. For instance, when $n = 2^2 \times 3 \times 5 = 60$, there are just over a thousand principal reversible squares; when $n = 2^2 \times 3^2 \times 5 \times 7 = 1260$ there are over one million; by the time n reaches $2^4 \times 3^3 \times 5^2 = 10{,}800$, the number has increased to over a billion (10^9) principal reversible squares (Table 7.3).

The total number of essentially different reversible squares, and hence also of essentially different most-perfect squares, is considerably larger, being $N_n M_n$, where

$$M_n = 2^{n-2}\{(\tfrac{1}{2}n)!\}^2 \qquad \text{from (2.4.2.1)},$$

is the number of reversible squares that can be derived from each principal reversible square by legitimate transformations. This shows that there are very large numbers of essentially different most-perfect squares, even for squares of small order n. For instance, even for n as small as 36, $M_{36} > 7 \times 10^{41}$ and there are more than 2×10^{44} essentially different most-perfect squares. This latter is a huge number, being more than a thousand times the number of pico-picoseconds since the Big Bang!

A personal perspective

Only now, with the work complete, is it possible for me to look back and see the process as it developed, savouring in retrospect the challenge presented when proof was first attempted, and recalling each step of the astonishing mathematical adventure that it has been. There was the extraordinary good fortune of capturing, almost by chance, the active interest of Professor David Brée, who offered to 'read' what I had done at a stage that I thought of as near-completion. His willingness to accept my invitation – at a late phase – to become co-author has added immeasurably to the value of the enterprise. In particular the enthusiasm with which Professor Brée took up my idea of extending the result to cover squares with sides of size n, where n is any integral multiple of 4 (whereas my original enumeration was for squares with more restricted values of n), has lifted the whole effort into a new category of endeavour – and, it is to be hoped, of mathematical signicance. New shorter methods were introduced, as well as clearer statements of lengthy arguments and improved nomenclatures – a process that could undoubtedly go on indefinitely were it not necessary to stop somewhere. Professor Brée has made a deep analysis of the substantial literature, especially that of the past hundred years, that is directly relevant to our own contribution to a much-ploughed field covering many centuries – a task that I, culpably, had largely neglected at a serious academic level. This involved a great deal of time and work, but helps, importantly, to place the present work in a proper historical perspective.

By 1988 I had found the enumeration for all squares here defined as most-perfect, first for values of $n = 2^r$ ($r > 1$) and subsequently for $n = 2^r p^s$ (p any prime > 2, $r > 1$, $s \geq 0$), purely by extrapolation of Eamon McClintock's ideas of 1897 that are detailed elsewhere. The result for $n = 2^r p^s$, now given as (6.7.2) in Chapter 6, was communicated to Martin Gardner in 1992. I had no proof, and the method seemed to give little hope of proof. After a gap of about four years, while walking my dogs in the local park and thinking about this 'unfinished business', the idea occurred to me of creating new squares (later named 'reversible') related to the McClintock squares. These are formed by blocks of consecutive integers embedded in larger blocks of increasing size. They held promise, now fulfilled, with substantial help from Professor Brée, of developing a logical proof for the enumeration of all pandiagonal magic squares of this particular type. Fortunately, the difficulties that were to be encountered en route to proof were not immediately apparent, but that is in the very nature of research – for once embarked upon there is no stopping, whatever the cost. We found later with surprise and delight, that the idea behind these reversible squares, that I had originally derived via McClintock, had been discovered and used by Barkley Rosser and R. J. Walker in their elegant and erudite paper of 1939. They called them 'normalized primitive squares' and used them in the construction of a variety of pandiagonal magic squares. (Rosser and Walker did not attempt a complete enumeration.) In a subject that has attracted the imagination of many mathematicians, both professional and lay, over so many years, it is almost inevitable that there should be some unconscious rediscovery of the wheel during the process of arriving at genuinely new results.

The key to the final enumeration lies in the triple product identity, quoted from *Concrete Mathematics* and labelled I.12 in Appendix A, that establishes a closed form for an equation that I had found by experiment was a step in an orderly progression that leads to the required totals. The equations did not emerge spontaneously but through hard work and growing familiarity with the requirements of the process of enumeration. The transformations required to relate the equations with I.12 inevitably somewhat disguise the processes by which the equations themselves were discovered.

The final stage of generalizing the enumeration to cover all values of n that are multiples of 4 was accomplished by Professor Brée. He also established that it is impossible to eliminate the index of summation from the formula that gives the enumeration for $n = 2^r p^s$. This is a disappointment: it would have been nice if the enumeration could have been expressed in terms of the given powers r and s alone.

The manner in which each successive application of the properties of binomial coefficients that characterize the Pascal triangle led to the solution will always remain one of the most magical mathematical revelations that I have been fortunate enough to experience. That this should be afforded to someone who had, with a few exceptions, been out of active mathematics research for over forty years will, I hope, encourage others. The delight of discovery is not a privilege reserved solely for the young.

KATHLEEN OLLERENSHAW
25 DECEMBER 1997

Glossary

This is a glossary of symbols and terms. The equation or section in which they are defined is indicated. Included are the symbols that occur with the same significance in more than one section. They are of three types: indices and variables, labels and functions. The definition given to terms is that appropriate to this work; it may be less general than would be found in a dictionary of such terms.

Indices and variables

f an integral factor of n, defining the position $(0, f)$ immediately before which the leftmost occurrence of the largest gap > 1 in the rows of a principal reversible square occur (Section 4.4.4); later restricted to $2^r p^{s'}$ (5.1.2.2).

f_1 a factor of f defining the position $(0, f_1)$ immediately before which the leftmost gap > 1 (if any) occurs in the rows of a principal reversible square (Section 4.2.2).

f_v the vth factor selected from a progressive path through the f-factor table, with 1 omitted (Section 4.1.2).

g index, $0 \le g \le n^2 / n_v f_v$, for a block, $B_g\,(n_v, f_v)$, similar to a corner block, $B_0\,(n_v, f_v)$ (Section 4.1.3).

i index, either for the row in a square $(0 \le i < n)$ (Sections 2.2.1, 2.3.2), or the number of steps in a progressive path through an f-factor table $(0 \le i < v)$ (Section 5.2.2).

i', i'' indices, $0 \le \{i', i''\} < n$, for particular rows in a reversible square (Section 2.4.1).

j index for the column of a square $(0 \le j < n)$ (Sections 2.2.1, 2.3.2).

j', j'' indices, $0 \le \{j', j''\} < n$, for particular columns in a reversible square (Section 2.4.1).

n	any modulo 4 integer ≥ 0; the order of a square (Section 2.2.1); later restricted to $2^r p^s$ (5.1.2.1).
n_1	a factor of n defining the position $(n_1, 0)$ immediately above which the first gap $> f_1$ (if any) occurs in the leftmost column of the completed principal reversible square (Section 4.2.2).
n_v	the vth factor selected from a progressive path through the n-factor table, with 1 omitted (Section 4.1.2).
p	any prime number > 2, as in $n = 2^r p^s$ (5.1.2.1).
r	any integer > 1; the power of 2, as in $n = 2^r p^s$ (5.1.2.1).
r'	integer, $0 \leq r' \leq r$, as in $f = 2^{r'} p^{s'}$ (5.1.2.2).
s	any integer ≥ 0; the power of p in $n = 2^r p^s$ (5.1.2.1).
s'	integer, $0 \leq s' \leq s$, as in $f = 2^{r'} p^{s'}$ (5.1.2.2).
t	the number of factors in a progressive path through the n-factor table, with 1 and n excluded: $t = r + s - 1$ (5.1.2.4).
t'	the number of factors in a progressive path through the f-factor table, with 1 and f excluded: $t' = r' + s' - 1$ (5.1.2.3).
v	the number of factors selected from a progressive path in a factor table (Section 5.1.1).
S	the sum of two complementary integers: $S = n^2 - 1$ (Section 2.2.1).

Labels

$B(n_v, f_v)$	a block of integers forming n_v partial rows and f_v partial columns within a square (Section 4.1.2).
$B_0(n_1, f_1)$	the smallest corner block of a principal reversible square, with the integer 0 in its top-left corner (Section 4.3).
$B_0(n, f)$	the largest corner block of a principal reversible square, with the integer 0 in its top-left corner (Section 4.4.4).
$B_g(n_v, f_v)$	a block similar to a corner block $B_0(n_v, f_v)$, with the integer $gn_v f_v$ in its top-left corner (Section 4.1.3).
$p_{i,j}$	the integer in the ith row and jth column of a most-perfect square P (Section 2.2.1).
$r_{i,j}$	the integer in the ith row and jth column of a reversible square R (Section 2.3.2).
(i, j)	the position in the ith row and jth column of a square or factor table.

Functions

$\binom{u}{v}$	binomial coefficients, i.e. the number of different ways of choosing v objects from u different objects without replacement: $\binom{u}{v} = u! / v! (v - u)!$ (Appendix A.1).
$F_n(f)$	the number of different configurations for the largest corner block $B_0(n, f)$ (5.1.2.5).
M_n	the number of essentially different squares in a set of reversible squares: $M_n = 2^{n-2}\{(\tfrac{1}{2}n)!\}^2$ (2.4.2.1).
$M_n N_n$	the total number of doubly-even reversible squares, and so of all most-perfect squares (Section 2.4.2).
N_n	the total number of principal reversible squares (6.1.1).
$W_v(x)$	the number of different ways of choosing v factors along a progressive path through an x-factor table, with 1 and x excluded (Sections 5.1.2, 7.1):

$$W_v(n) = \begin{cases} \sum_j \binom{r}{j}\binom{s}{j}\binom{t-j}{v-j}, & \text{when } n = 2^r p^s; & (5.2.4.1) \\ \sum_i (-1)^{v+i} \binom{v+1}{i+1} \prod_g \binom{s_g+i}{i}, & \text{when } n = \prod_g p_g^{s_g}. & (7.1.6) \end{cases}$$

Definition of terms

Algorithm: a mechanical procedure for solving a problem in a finite number of steps.

Array: a set of integers arranged in a rectangle forming part of a square.
　　2 × 2: integers in four adjacent positions in a most-perfect square (Section 2.2.1).

Binomial: a polynomial consisting of two terms, for example, $x + y$.

Binomial coefficient: the coefficients of x^v in the expansion of $(1 + x)^u$; also the number of ways of choosing v objects from u different objects, without repetition, denoted by $\binom{u}{v}$ (Appendix A.1).

Block: a rectangular array of n_v rows and f_v columns within a principal reversible square, composed of $n_v f_v$ integers, arranged in ascending order (Section 4.1.2).
　　Building procedure: procedure by which larger blocks are built up from selected smaller blocks by using the 'layering process' (Section 4.4.3).
　　Corner: block with 0 in its top left corner consisting of the integers 0 to $n_v f_v - 1$ arranged in n_v partial rows and f_v partial columns of a principal reversible square, in ascending order (Section 4.1.3).
　　　Largest: the corner block, $B_0(n, f)$, in which $nf - f + 1$ is the largest gap in any row of the principal reversible square (Section 4.4.4).

Smallest: the corner block, B_0 (n_1, f_1), with no gap > 1 in its rows and no gap $> f_1$ in its columns (Section 4.2.2).

Similar: see 'Similar blocks'.

Column: the integers in a column of a square. The *j*th column includes integers at all positions $(i, j), 0 \leq i < n$.

Even: a column with an even label: $0, 2, \ldots , (n - 2)$.

Odd: a column with an odd label: $1, 3, \ldots , (n - 1)$.

Combinatorics/combinatorial mathematics: the study of arrangements of elements. It is particularly concerned with finding out whether an arrangement that meets specified requirements is possible, and if so, how many such arrangements are possible.

Complements: pairs of integers that add to a particular sum, e.g. to S.

Complementary: two integers are said to be complementary when they form complements.

Composite integer: an integer that is a product of two or more prime factors.

Counting numbers: $1, 2, 3, 4, \ldots$.

Couplets: pairs of integers in adjacent positions within a square.

Horizontal: when both integers lie in the same row (Section 2.2.3).

Vertical: when both integers lie in the same column (Section 1.4).

Diagonals:

Principal: the two diagonals within a square that run from the top-left corner to the bottom-right corner or from the bottom-left corner to the top-right corner.

Broken: are given by the positions $(i, (i + h) \bmod n)$ for all $0 \leq i < n$ (2.2.2.3).

Equal cross sums:

in an array: pairs of integers at opposite corners of any array within a reversible square have the same sum (2.3.2.3).

of two similar series of integers, a_v's and b_v's: $a_i + b_j = a_j + b_i$ (Section 2.3.1).

Essentially different square: see 'Squares, essentially different'.

Factor table: the factors of any composite integer, say $2^{r^*} p^{s^*}$, arranged in an array of $s^* + 1$ rows and $r^* + 1$ columns (Table 5.2).

Gap: the difference between any two adjacent integers within a row or within a column of a principal reversible square. The minimum gap is therefore 1. All other gaps are > 1.

Integer: the counting numbers, together with their negatives and zero.

Latin squares: squares of order n containing n different symbols, here the integers $0, 1, \ldots, (n - 1)$, arranged in such a way that each symbol occurs once and once only in each row and in each column. The sum of each row and column is then $\frac{1}{2}n(n-1)$ (Section 1.2).

Diagonal: are Latin squares in which the two principal diagonals also contain each symbol once and once only.

Orthogonal: are a pair of Latin squares, A and A', of the same order, n, in which the pairs of integers in each position are unique, i.e. the pairs $(a_{i,j}, a'_{i,j})$ are different for all $0 \le \{i, j\} < n$.

Pandiagonal: are diagonal Latin squares in which the sum of all integers in any diagonal, broken as well as principal, sum to $\frac{1}{2}n(n-1)$ (Section 1.3.1).

Self-orthogonal: are Latin squares, A, which are orthogonal to their transpose, A', i.e. $a'_{i,j} = a_{j,i}$.

Layer: consists of blocks, $B_g(n_v, f_v)$, similar to a corner block, placed side by side, without overlapping, to cover n_v adjacent rows from column 0 up to the next largest gap in the top row (Section 4.4.3); if the blocks are similar to the largest corner block, $B_0(n, f)$, then the layer covers up to the full width of the square (Section 4.5).

Layering process: placing layers of similar blocks, $B_g(n_v, f_v)$, each layer covering the next n_v rows below the previous layer and the same columns as the previous layer down to the next largest gap in column 0 (Section 4.4.3).

Modulo: a number modulo n is equal to i if, when the number is divided by n, it has a remainder i.

One-to-one correspondence: a mapping between two sets in which each member of either set is paired with one and only one member of the other set. The two sets must have the same number of members.

Order: the number of rows (and columns) in a square.

Path: (r, c) in an auxiliary square is a sequence of n positions in the square linked in such a way that moving r rows down and c columns along from one position leads to the next position. Either r or c is equal to 1 (Section 1.3.2).

Knight's: the path through the square made by a chess knight moving in the same direction throughout the square, i.e. the paths $(1, \pm 2)$ or $(2, \pm 1)$.

Non-intersecting: those paths that intersect only in their common starting position.

Permissible: paths returning to their starting position in n moves.

Progressive: see 'Progressive path'.

Prime: an integer, other than 0, +1, −1, not evenly divisible by an integer except itself (plus or minus) and 1 (plus or minus). The first positive primes are 2, 3, 5, 7, 11, 13, 17, 19, ...

Progressive:

factors: a series of factors such that each factor is an integral multiple of all lesser factors in the series (Section 4.4.4). When $n = 2^r p^s$ they lie along a progressive path.

path: a progression through the integers of an x-factor table that moves from one position to the next, either by moving horizontally one position at a time along a row from left to right, or vertically down a column. The next factor is always a multiple of the previous factor and either 2 or p. A progressive path starts at 1, in the top-left corner, either going along the top row or down the leftmost column, and ends at x, in the bottom right-hand corner. The progression is thus always 'downhill' (Section 5.2.1).

Reflections: in the horizontal or vertical axes or in either of the principal diagonals; when applied to a square the resulting square is not essentially different from the original (Section 1.1). In a square, reflections exchange the integer at positions (i, j), $0 \leq \{i, j\} < n$, with the integer at position (Section 2.4.1):

$r_{n-1-i,j}$ or $r_{i,n-1-j}$, for reflection in the horizontal or vertical axes, respectively;

$r_{j,i}$ or $r_{n-1-j,n-1-i}$, for reflection in the two principal diagonals;

$r_{n-1-i,n-1-j}$ for reflection in the mid-point.

Reverse similarity: two sequences are said to be in reverse similarity when, if the second sequence is reversed, the sum of integers in the same position is constant (Section 2.3.1).

Reversible squares: squares in which all rows and all columns have reverse similarity in the vertical and the horizontal axes, respectively, and all arrays have equal cross sums (Section 2.3.2).

Doubly-even: a reversible square of doubly-even order, i.e. n modulo $4 = 0$.

Principal: reversible squares with integers in all rows/columns in ascending order, the top row starting with 0 1 (Section 2.5).

Legitimate transformations of: see 'Transformations, legitimate'.

Row: the integers in a row of a square. The ith row includes integers at all positions (i, j), $0 \leq j < n$.

Even: a row with an even label: $0, 2, \dots , (n - 2)$.

Odd: a row with an odd label: $1, 3, \dots , (n - 1)$.

S-complements: two integers that sum to S.

Set: any collection of identifiable like items, such as squares of a particular type.

Similar: sequences of integers $a_0, a_1, \dots , a_{h-1}, a_h$ and $b_0, b_1 \dots , b_{h-1}, b_h$ are similar when the difference between integers in the same position in both sequences is constant: $a_i - b_i = a_j - b_j, 0 \leq \{i, j\} \leq h$ (Section 2.3.1).

blocks: two blocks are similar when they have the same dimensions and each row/column of one block is similar to the corresponding row/column of the other block, e.g. if the block, $B_g(n_v, f_v)$, is similar to the corner block, $B_0(n_v, f_v)$, then the integer gn_vf_v in its top-left corner defines the block (Section 4.1.3).

rows/columns: when the integers that comprise a pair of rows/columns are similar, the rows/columns are similar.

Squares:

Auxiliary: a pair of squares of order n that are orthogonal, such that, when one (usually first being multiplied by n) is added to the other, the result is a magic square of order n (Section 1.2).

    Mixed: a pair of auxiliary squares that are directly summed (rather than one of them first being multiplied by n) to form a pandiagonal magic square (Section 1.2).

    Radix: the auxiliary that is multiplied by n before being added to the unit auxiliary to form a magic square (Section 1.2).

    Unit: the auxiliary that is not multiplied by n before being added to the radix auxiliary to form a magic square (Section 1.2).

Essentially different: squares are essentially different if they cannot be transformed into one another by any combination of reflections (Section 2.4.2).

Magic: squares in which all rows and columns and the two principal diagonals have the same sum, being $\frac{1}{2}n(n^2 - 1)$ for normal squares (Section 1.1).

McClintock: squares of order n containing n^2 consecutive integers arranged in such a way that all even rows are similar, all odd rows are similar and, for any pair of adjacent rows, all vertical couplets have a constant sum. Also, pairs of integers a distance $\frac{1}{2}n$ along a diagonal add to $(n^2 - 1)$ (Section 1.4).

Most-perfect: pandiagonal magic squares in which integers forming 2×2 arrays add to the same sum, being $2(n^2 - 1)$ for normal squares, and in which pairs of integers a distance $\frac{1}{2}n$ along a diagonal add to $(n^2 - 1)$ (Section 2.2.1).

Normal: squares of order n comprising the consecutive integers 0 to $(n^2 - 1)$ (Section 1.1).

Primitive: squares with the property of 'equal cross sums', but not necessarily with the other properties of reversible squares. 'Normalized primitive squares' are primitive squares with integers in all rows/columns in ascending order, with the top row starting with the two smallest integers (Section 1.3.5).

Pandiagonal: magic squares in which all diagonals (the principal as well as broken diagonals) have the same sum, being $\frac{1}{2}n\,(n^2 - 1)$ for normal squares (Section 1.1).

Reversible: see 'Reversible squares'.

Step: position in a progressive path where the direction changes from horizontal to vertical, i.e. the factor in this position is 2 times the previous factor and $1/p$ times the next factor in the path (Section 5.2.2).

Transformation: of a doubly-even reversible square into a most-perfect square (Section 3.1.1):

Legitimate: transformations that leave reversible squares still reversible squares (Section 2.4.1).

Inverse: transformation of most-perfect squares into reversible squares (Section 3.2.1).

Appendix A
Properties of binomial coefficients

A.1 Definitions

The binomial coefficient is defined by the expressions

$$\binom{\rho}{i} = \begin{cases} \rho(\rho - 1) \dots (\rho - i + 1)/i! & \text{integer } i \geq 0, \\ 0 & \text{integer } i < 0, \end{cases} \qquad (CM\ 5.1)$$

where ρ is called the *upper index* and i is called the *lower index*. When ρ is an integer α, this has a combinatorial interpretation representing the number of ways of choosing i objects from α objects, namely $\alpha\ (\alpha - 1)\ (\alpha - 2) \dots (\alpha - i + 1)/i!$ when $i \geq 0$.

These binomial coefficients can be arranged to form the *Pascal triangle*[*] (Blaise Pascal, 1623–1662). The triangle has at its apex the single digit 1. Integers are then arranged in rows of increasing width, each row starting and ending with 1 and each element within the rows being the sum of the two integers immediately to the left and to the right in the row above. The elements of the triangle are given by:

Pascal triangle

$$\binom{\alpha}{i} = \frac{\alpha!}{i!\,(\alpha - i)!}, \qquad \text{integers } \alpha \geq i \geq 0. \qquad (CM\ 5.3)$$

The *extended Pascal triangle* or, as Sir Isaac Newton (1642−1727), its discoverer, aptly described it, the 'backward extension', widens the definition given above to include

$$\binom{\alpha}{i} = (-1)^i \binom{i - \alpha - 1}{i}, \qquad \text{integers } \alpha,\ i. \qquad (CM\ 5.14)$$

[*] A pictorial representation of the Pascal triangle is given in Appendix A.3.

The relationship between the extended Pascal triangle and the Pascal triangle itself is illustrated below in a joint table used by Stuart Hollingdale (1989) in *Makers of mathematics*, page 182:

Newton's backward extension						Pascal							
1	1	1	1	1		1	1	1	1	1	1	1	1 ...
−5	−4	−3	−2	−1		0	1	2	3	4	5	6	7 ...
15	10	6	3	1		0	0	1	3	6	10	15	21 ...
−35	−20	−10	−4	−1		0	0	0	1	4	10	20	35 ...
70	35	15	5	1		0	0	0	0	1	5	15	35 ...
−125	−56	−21	−6	−1		0	0	0	0	0	1	6	21 ...
210	84	28	7	1		0	0	0	0	0	0	1	7 ...

In the joint table above, a new entry is computed as:
- for Newton's backward extension: the entry immediately to the right less the entry immediately above, e.g. −35 = (−20) − 15;
- for the Pascal triangle: the entry immediately to the left plus the entry immediately above that, e.g. 20 = 10 + 10.

The coefficients in the expansion of $(1 + x)^n$ are obtained by reading down the column whose second entry is n, e.g.:

$$(1 + x)^{-4} = 1 - 4x + 10x^2 - 20x^3 + 35x^4 - 56x^5 + 84x^6 \ldots ;$$
$$(1 + x)^6 = 1 + 6x + 15x^2 + 20x^3 + 15x^4 + 6x^5 + x^6.$$

A.2 A list of binomial coefficient identities

A.2.1 Outline of the list

The binomial coefficient identities listed below, I.1 to I.13, some of which are extensively used in Chapter 6, are taken without further proof from Chapter 5 of *Concrete mathematics* (Graham, Knuth and Patashnik, 1989). The alphabetical characters in the original text are here replaced by their Greek equivalents to avoid confusion with the symbols used with special connotations in the main text. In particular the characters l, m, n, r, s are replaced by λ, μ, ν, ρ, σ; and k in *Concrete mathematics* is replaced here by i. Identities that are quoted from *Concrete mathematics* are labelled by the equation numberings used there, preceded by '*CM*'.

A.2.2 The list

I.1: *Symmetry*

$$\binom{\nu}{i} = \binom{\nu}{\nu - i}, \qquad \text{integer } \nu \geq 0; \text{ integer } i. \qquad (CM\ 5.4)$$

$$p_{0,j} + p_{\frac{1}{2}n,j} + p_{1,j} + p_{1 + \frac{1}{2}n,j} = 2S. \tag{2.2.3.2}$$

The proof is similar to the previous proof. Note that the integers in a horizontal couplet in the right half of a row are both S-complements of the integers in a horizontal couplet situated in a row $\frac{1}{2}n$ down (or up) covering adjacent columns distant $\frac{1}{2}n$ from the original pair. Now the sum of this complementary couplet is the same as the sum of the horizontal couplet in the same columns but in a row $\frac{1}{2}n$ up (or down), i.e. in the original row, since $\frac{1}{2}n$ is even (B.2.1). So the sum of any horizontal couplet, plus the sum of the couplet distant $\frac{1}{2}n$ along the same row, is $2S$. By taking two such couplets with one position in common, the proof of (2.3.3.1) follows.

Let the common position be in column j^*; then:

$$p_{i,j^* - 1 + \frac{1}{2}n} + p_{i,j^* + \frac{1}{2}n} = 2S - (p_{i + \frac{1}{2}n,j^* - 1} + p_{i + \frac{1}{2}n,j^*}) \quad \text{by (2.2.1.2) twice}$$

$$= 2S - (p_{i,j^* - 1} + p_{i,j^*}) \quad \text{by (B.2.1), as } \tfrac{1}{2}n \text{ is even.}$$

Similarly,

$$p_{i,j^* + \frac{1}{2}n} + p_{i,j^* + 1 + \frac{1}{2}n} = 2S - (p_{i,j^*} + p_{i,j^* + 1}).$$

Subtracting:

$$p_{i,j^* - 1} + p_{i,j^* - 1 + \frac{1}{2}n} = p_{i,j^* + 1} + p_{i,j^* + 1 + \frac{1}{2}n}.$$

Substituting:

$j^* = 2j + 1$, $\quad p_{i,2j} + p_{i,2j + \frac{1}{2}n} = p_{i,2j + 2} + p_{i,2j + 2 + \frac{1}{2}n},$

$j^* = 2j$, $\quad p_{i,2j - 1} + p_{i,2j - 1 + \frac{1}{2}n} = p_{i,2j + 1} + p_{i,2j + 1 + \frac{1}{2}n},$

$j^* = 0$, $\quad p_{i,0} + p_{i,\frac{1}{2}n} + p_{i,1} + p_{i,1 + \frac{1}{2}n} = 2S \quad$ (from four lines above);

these together prove (2.2.3.1).

The proof of (2.2.3.2) for columns proceeds likewise. Let the common position be in row i^*; then:

$$p_{i^* - 1 + \frac{1}{2}n,j} + p_{i^* + \frac{1}{2}n,j} = 2S - (p_{i^* - 1,j + \frac{1}{2}n} + p_{i^*,j + \frac{1}{2}n}) \quad \text{by (2.2.1.2) twice}$$

$$= 2S - (p_{i^* - 1,j} + p_{i^*,j}) \quad \text{by (B.2.1), as } \tfrac{1}{2}n \text{ is even.}$$

Similarly,

$$p_{i^* + \frac{1}{2}n,j} + p_{i^* + 1 + \frac{1}{2}n,j} = 2S - (p_{i^*,j} + p_{i^* + 1,j}).$$

Subtracting:

$$p_{i^* - 1,j} + p_{i^* - 1 + \frac{1}{2}n,j} = p_{i^*+1,j} + p_{i^* + 1 + \frac{1}{2}n,j}.$$

Substituting:

$i^* = 2i + 1$, $\quad p_{2i,j} + p_{2i + \frac{1}{2}n,j} = p_{2i + 2,j} + p_{2i + 2 + \frac{1}{2}n,j},$

$i^* = 2i$, $\quad p_{2i - 1,j} + p_{2i - 1 + \frac{1}{2}n,j} = p_{2i + 1,j} + p_{2i + 1 + \frac{1}{2}n,j},$

$i^* = 0$, $\quad p_{0,j} + p_{\frac{1}{2}n,j} + p_{1,j} + p_{1 + \frac{1}{2}n,j} = 2S \quad$ (from four lines above);

these together prove (2.2.3.2).

B.3 The sum of any pair of integers reflected in the mid-point of a reversible square is S

The proof that the sum of any pair of integers that are reflections in the mid-point of a reversible square is $S = (n^2 - 1)$ (2.3.3.4), i.e. that

$$r_{i,j} + r_{n-1-i,\,n-1-j} = S$$

begins by showing that their sum is constant and then shows that this constant must be S.

As an illustration of the detailed proof, the method is demonstrated by showing that the sum of pairs of integers in the main diagonal of the square

$$
\begin{array}{cccc}
0 & 1 & 2 & 3 \\
4 & 5 & 6 & 7 \\
8 & 9 & 10 & 11 \\
12 & 13 & 14 & 15
\end{array}
$$

that are at positions reflected in the mid-point is constant, using only the definitional properties of the reversible square. That is so say, show for example that $0 + 15 = 5 + 10$, without using simple arithmetic! Note that by equal cross sums (2.3.2.3): $5 + 10 = 6 + 9$, $4 + 11 = 8 + 7$ and $3 + 12 = 0 + 15$. By reverse similarity of:

rows 1 and 2:	columns 0 and 4:
$4 + 7 = 5 + 6$	$4 + 8 = 0 + 12$
$8 + 11 = 9 + 10$	$7 + 11 = 3 + 15$

Adding: $4 + 11 + 8 + 7 = 5 + 10 + 6 + 9,$ $4 + 11 + 8 + 7 = 0 + 15 + 3 + 12,$
By (2.3.2.3), $2(4 + 11) = 2(5 + 10)$ $2(4 + 11) = 2(0 + 15),$
So $5 + 10 = 4 + 11 = 0 + 15$, as required. The proof in general follows.

Note that, by equal cross sums (2.3.2.3) in three different arrays, sharing two pairs of rows, i and i', and two pairs of columns, j and j':

$$r_{i,j} + r_{n-1-i,\,n-1-j} = r_{n-1-i,j} + r_{i,\,n-1-j}, \tag{B.3.1}$$

$$r_{i,j'} + r_{n-1-i,\,n-1-j'} = r_{n-1-i,j'} + r_{i,\,n-1-j'}, \tag{B.3.2}$$

$$r_{i',j'} + r_{n-1-i',\,n-1-j'} = r_{n-1-i',j'} + r_{i',\,n-1-j'}. \tag{B.3.3}$$

By reverse similarity of rows i and $n - 1 - i$:

$$r_{i,j} + r_{i,\,n-1-j} = r_{i,j'} + r_{i,\,n-1-j'} \quad \text{and}$$

$$r_{n-1-i,j} + r_{n-1-i,\,n-1-j} = r_{n-1-i,j'} + r_{n-1-i,\,n-1-j'}.$$

By addition and by substitution from (B.3.1) and (B.3.2):

$$2(r_{i,j} + r_{n-1-i,\,n-1-j}) = 2(r_{i,j'} + r_{n-1-i,\,n-1-j'}). \tag{B.3.4}$$

By reverse similarity of columns j' and $n - 1 - j'$:

$$r_{i,j'} + r_{n-1-i,j'} = r_{i',j'} + r_{n-1-i',j'} \quad \text{and}$$

$$r_{i,\,n-1-j'} + r_{n-1-i,\,n-1-j'} = r_{i',\,n-1-j'} + r_{n-1-i',\,n-1-j'}.$$

By addition and by substitution from (B.3.2) and (B.3.3):

$$2\left(r_{i,j'} + r_{n-1-i,\,n-1-j'}\right) = 2\left(r_{i',j} + r_{n-1-i',\,n-1-j}\right). \qquad (B.3.5)$$

Combining (B.3.4) and (B.3.5) gives:

$$r_{i,j} + r_{n-1-i,\,n-1-j} = r_{i',j} + r_{n-1-i',\,n-1-j'}.$$

Hence the sum of any pair of integers reflected in the mid-point is constant. There are $\frac{1}{2}n^2$ such pairs and the total sum over all integers is $\frac{1}{2}n^2\,(n^2-1)$, so each pair sums to $(n^2-1) = S$, which proves (2.3.3.4).

B.4 Proofs of the legitimate transformations

It needs to be proved that the legitimate transformations of a reversible square result in a square that is also reversible. These transformations are: reflection in either the vertical or horizontal axis, reflection in either of the principal diagonals, interchanging pairs of complementary rows or columns and, finally, interchanging two rows/columns in one half of the square as well as their complementary rows/columns in the other half.

Let $q_{i,j}$ denote the integers in the position (i, j) of the square into which the reversible square has been transformed. The proof will show that the transformed squares satisfy the three definitional properties of a reversible square, namely that the rows and columns have reverse similarity (2.3.2.1, 2.3.2.2) and that any array has equal cross sums (2.3.2.3):

$$q_{i,j} + q_{i,\,n-1-j} = q_{i,j'} + q_{i,\,n-1-j'},$$

$$q_{i,j} + q_{n-1-i,\,j} = q_{i',j} + q_{n-1-i',\,j},$$

$$q_{i,j} + q_{i',j'} = q_{i,j'} + q_{i',j}.$$

B.4.1 Reflection about the vertical axis

For reflection about the vertical axis $q_{i,j} = r_{i,\,n-1-j}$ (2.4.1.1). The $q_{i,j}$ then form a reversible square, since:

(i) the rows have reverse similarity, as:

$$q_{i,j} + q_{i,\,n-1-j} = r_{i,\,n-1-j} + r_{i,j} = r_{i,\,n-1-j'} + r_{i,j'} \quad \text{by (2.3.2.1)}$$
$$= q_{i,j'} + q_{i,\,n-1-j'};$$

(ii) the columns still have reverse similarity as they have not been changed;

(iii) all arrays have equal cross sums, as:

$$q_{i,j} + q_{i',j'} = r_{i,\,n-1-j} + r_{i',\,n-1-j'} = r_{i,\,n-1-j'} + r_{i',\,n-1-j} \quad \text{by (2.3.2.3)}$$
$$= q_{i,j'} + q_{i',j}.$$

B.4.2 Reflection about the horizontal axis

For reflection about the horizontal axis $q_{i,j} = r_{n-1-i,j}$ (2.4.1.2). The $q_{i,j}$ then form a reversible square, since:

(i) the rows still have reverse similarity as they have not been changed;

(ii) the columns have reverse similarity, as:

$$q_{i,j} + q_{n-1-i,j} = r_{n-1-i,j} + r_{i,j} = r_{n-1-i',j} + r_{i',j} \quad \text{by (2.3.2.2)}$$
$$= q_{i',j} + q_{n-1-i',j};$$

(iii) all arrays have equal cross sums as:

$$q_{i,j} + q_{i',j'} = r_{n-1-i,j} + r_{n-1-i',j'} = r_{n-1-i,j'} + r_{n-1-i',j} \quad \text{by (2.3.2.3)}$$
$$= q_{i,j'} + q_{i',j}.$$

B.4.3 Reflection about the major principal diagonal

For reflection about the major principal diagonal $q_{i,j} = r_{j,i}$ (2.4.1.3). The $q_{i,j}$ then form a reversible square, since:

(i) the rows have reverse similarity, as:

$$q_{i,j} + q_{i,n-1-j} = r_{j,i} + r_{n-1-j,i} = r_{j',i} + r_{n-1-j',i} \quad \text{by (2.3.2.2)}$$
$$= q_{i,j'} + q_{i,n-1-j'};$$

(ii) the columns have reverse similarity, as:

$$q_{i,j} + q_{n-1-i,j} = r_{j,i} + r_{j,n-1-i} = r_{j,i'} + r_{j,n-1-i'} \quad \text{by (2.3.2.1)}$$
$$= q_{i',j} + q_{n-1-i',j};$$

(iii) all arrays have equal cross sums, as:

$$q_{i,j} + q_{i',j'} = r_{j,i} + r_{j',i'} = r_{j,i'} + r_{j',i} \quad \text{by (2.3.2.3)}$$
$$= q_{i,j'} + q_{i',j}.$$

B.4.4 Reflection about the minor principal diagonal

For reflection about the minor principal diagonal $q_{i,j} = r_{n-1-j,n-1-i}$ (2.4.1.4). The $q_{i,j}$ then form a reversible square, since:

(i) the rows have reverse similarity, as:

$$q_{i,j} + q_{i,n-1-j} = r_{n-1-j,n-1-i} + r_{j,n-1-i} = r_{n-1-j',n-1-i} + r_{j',n-1-i}$$
$$\text{by (2.3.2.2)}$$
$$= q_{i,j'} + q_{i,n-1-j'};$$

(ii) the columns have reverse similarity, as:

$$q_{i,j} + q_{n-1-i,j} = r_{n-1-j,n-1-i} + r_{n-1-j,i} = r_{n-1-j,n-1-i'} + r_{n-1-j,i'}$$
$$\text{by (2.3.2.1)}$$

$$= q_{i',j} + q_{n-1-i',j};$$

(iii) all arrays have equal cross sums, as:

$$q_{i,j} + q_{i',j'} = r_{n-1-j,n-1-i} + r_{n-1-j',n-1-i'}$$

$$= r_{n-1-j,n-1-i'} + r_{n-1-j',n-1-i} \quad \text{by (2.3.2.3)}$$

$$= q_{i,j'} + q_{i',j}.$$

B.4.5 Interchanging complementary pairs of rows

To interchange a complementary pair of rows, let:

$$q_{i^*,j} = r_{n-1-i^*,j} \quad \text{and} \quad q_{n-1-i^*,j} = r_{i^*,j} \quad \text{for any one value of } i^* \text{ and}$$

$$q_{i,j} = r_{i,j} \quad \text{for all } i \neq \{i^*, (n-1-i^*)\} \quad (2.4.1.5).$$

Then:

(i) The rows still have reverse similarity as they have not been changed.

(ii) The columns have reverse similarity as the only change is to interchange a pair of complementary integers in each column. In detail, for $\{i, i'\} \neq \{i^*, (n-1-i^*)\}$:

$$q_{i,j} + q_{n-1-i,j} = r_{i,j} + r_{n-1-i,j} = r_{i',j} + r_{n-1-i',j} \quad \text{by (2.3.2.2)}$$

$$= q_{i',j} + q_{n-1-i',j};$$

$$q_{i^*,j} + q_{n-1-i^*,j} = r_{n-1-i^*,j} + r_{i^*,j} = r_{n-1-i,j} + r_{i,j} \quad \text{by (2.3.2.2)}$$

$$= q_{i,j} + q_{n-1-i,j}.$$

(iii) All arrays have equal cross sums. Consider the more general case of interchanging any two rows i^* and i''. First, the corners of arrays that are not on any of the interchanged rows are not affected. If only two corners fall in the interchanged rows, say row i*, but the other two corners do not, then

$$q_{i^*,j} + q_{i,j'} = r_{i'',j} + r_{i,j'} = r_{i'',j'} + r_{i,j} \quad \text{by (2.3.2.3)}$$

$$= q_{i^*,j'} + q_{i,j} \quad \text{for } i \neq \{i^*, i''\}. \quad (\text{B.4.5.1})$$

If all four corners of the array fall in the two interchanged rows, i.e. into rows i^* and i'', then:

$$q_{i^*,j} + q_{i'',j'} = r_{i'',j} + r_{i^*,j'} = r_{i'',j'} + r_{i^*,j} \quad \text{by (2.3.2.3)}$$

$$= q_{i^*,j'} + q_{i'',j}. \quad (\text{B.4.5.2})$$

This covers all possibilities of the position of the array with respect to the pair of interchanged rows. Therefore the property of equal cross sums is invariant under row interchange (see also Rosser and Walker, 1939). In particular (B.4.5.1) and (B.4.5.2) hold for $i'' = n - 1 - i^*$.

Hence the $q_{i,j}$ form a reversible square.

B.4.6 Interchanging complementary pairs of columns

To interchange a complementary pair of columns, let:

$$q_{i,j^*} = r_{i,n-1-j^*} \quad \text{and} \quad q_{i,n-1-j^*} = r_{i,j^*} \quad \text{for any one value of } j^* \text{ and}$$
$$q_{i,j} = r_{i,j} \quad \text{for all } j \neq \{j^*, (n-1-j^*)\} \quad (2.4.1.6).$$

Then:

(i) The rows have reverse similarity as the only change is to interchange a pair of complementary integers in each row. In detail, for $\{j, j'\} \neq \{j^*, (n-1-j^*)\}$:

$$q_{i,j} + q_{i,n-1-j} = r_{i,j} + r_{i,n-1-j} = r_{i,j'} + r_{i,n-1-j'} \quad \text{by (2.3.2.1)}$$
$$= q_{i,j'} + q_{i,n-1-j'};$$

$$q_{i,j^*} + q_{i,n-1-j^*} = r_{i,n-1-j^*} + r_{i,j^*} = r_{i,n-1-j} + r_{i,j} \quad \text{by (2.3.2.1)}$$
$$= q_{i,j} + q_{i,n-1-j}.$$

(ii) The columns still have reverse similarity as they have not been changed.

(iii) All arrays have equal cross sums. Consider the more general case of interchanging any two columns j^* and j''. First, the corners of arrays that are not on any of the interchanged columns are not affected. If only two corners fall in the interchanged columns, say column j^*, but the other two corners do not, then:

$$q_{i,j^*} + q_{i',j} = r_{i,j''} + r_{i',j} = r_{i,j} + r_{i',j''} \quad \text{by (2.3.2.3)}$$
$$= q_{i,j} + q_{i',j^*} \quad \text{for } j \neq \{j^*, j''\}. \tag{B.4.6.1}$$

If all four corners of the array fall in the two interchanged columns, i.e. into columns j^* and j'', then:

$$q_{i,j^*} + q_{i',j''} = r_{i,j''} + r_{i',j^*} = r_{i,j^*} + r_{i',j''} \quad \text{by (2.3.2.3)}$$
$$= q_{i,j''} + q_{i',j^*}. \tag{B.4.6.2}$$

This covers all possibilities of the position of the array with respect to the pair of interchanged columns. Therefore the property of equal cross sums is invariant under column interchange (see also Rosser and Walker, 1939). In particular (B.4.6.1) and (B.4.6.2) hold for $j'' = n - 1 - j^*$.

Hence the $q_{i,j}$ form a reversible square.

B.4.7 Interchanging two rows in one half of the square and their complementary pair of rows in the other half

To interchange two rows, i^* and i'', in one half of the square and at the same time to interchange the complementary pair of rows in the other half of the square, let:

$$q_{i^*,j} = r_{i'',j} \quad \text{and} \quad q_{i'',j} = r_{i^*,j},$$

$$q_{n-1-i^*,j} = r_{n-1-i'',j} \quad \text{and} \quad q_{n-1-i'',j} = r_{n-1-i^*,j},$$

$$q_{i,j} = r_{i,j} \quad \text{for } i \neq \{i^*, i'', (n-1-i^*), (n-1-i'')\} \quad (2.4.1.7).$$

Then:

(i) The rows still have reverse similarity as they have not been changed.

(ii) The columns have reverse similarity as the only change to the upper half of each column is matched by an interchange of the integers in symmetrical positions in the bottom half. In detail, for $\{i, i'\} \neq \{i^*, i'', (n-1-i^*), (n-1-i'')\}$:

$$q_{i,j} + q_{n-1-i,j} = r_{i,j} + r_{n-1-i,j} = r_{i',j} + r_{n-1-i',j} \quad \text{by (2.3.2.2)}$$

$$= q_{i',j} + q_{n-1-i',j};$$

$$q_{i^*,j} + q_{n-1-i^*,j} = r_{i'',j} + r_{n-1-i'',j} = r_{i,j} + r_{n-1-i,j} \quad \text{by (2.3.2.2)}$$

$$= q_{i,j} + q_{n-1-i,j};$$

$$q_{i'',j} + q_{n-1-i'',j} = r_{i^*,j} + r_{n-1-i^*,j} = r_{i,j} + r_{n-1-i,j} \quad \text{by (2.3.2.2)}$$

$$= q_{i,j} + q_{n-1-i,j}.$$

(iii) The property of equal cross sums is invariant under both row exchanges (B.4.5.1, B.4.5.2). Therefore all arrays have equal cross sums.

Hence the $q_{i,j}$ form a reversible square.

B.4.8 Interchanging two columns in one half of the square and their complementary pairs of columns in the other half

To interchange two columns, j^* and j'', in one half of the square and at the same time to interchange the complementary pair of columns in the other half of the square, let:

$$q_{i,j^*} = r_{i,j''} \quad \text{and} \quad q_{i,j''} = r_{i,j^*},$$

$$q_{i,n-1-j^*} = r_{i,n-1-j''} \quad \text{and} \quad q_{i,n-1-j''} = r_{i,n-1-j^*},$$

$$q_{i,j} = r_{i,j} \quad \text{for } j \neq \{j^*, j'', (n-1-j^*), (n-1-j'')\} \quad (2.4.1.8).$$

The proof that the $q_{i,j}$ form a reversible square proceeds similarly to the proof for interchanging two pairs of rows (Section B.4.7).

B.5 Another feature of most-perfect squares

A feature of all most-perfect squares with $n > 4$ is that there are at least two occurrences of 0 in one row of either one or the other of their auxiliary squares. To show this, consider all reversible squares that can be reached by legitimate transformations from a principal reversible square. The integer at the position (0, 2) of the principal reversible square must be either $< n$ or n or $2n$ (Section 8.1).

If the integer at (0, 2) is $< n$, there are then three integers $< n$ in the top row of the principal reversible square: 0, 1 and this integer at (0, 2). If the principal reversible square is transformed into any other reversible square in its set, all integers in any row will always be in a row after transformation (Section 2.4.1), so these three integers will be found together in the same row, for any reversible square. When the reversible square is transformed, by using (3.1.1.5), into a most-perfect square, the integers in any row of the reversible square will be moved to one of two rows of the most-perfect square, depending on whether they come from an even or an odd column. This can be most easily seen by inspection of the inverse transformation (3.2.1.4). As all three integers are $< n$, one row (or possibly more than one) of the most-perfect square has at least two integers $< n$. Consequently, the radix auxiliary from which the most-perfect square is composed has at least two occurrences of 0 in one of its rows.

If the integer at the position (0, 2) in the principal reversible square is not $< n$ but either n or $2n$, then, for $n > 4$, the integer at the position (0, 4) must be $2n$ or $4n$, respectively. By a similar argument to that used in the previous paragraph, it can be shown that two of the three integers 0, n and $2n$ (or 0, $2n$ and $4n$) lie in the same row for every most-perfect square that is the transformation, by using (3.1.1.5), of any reversible square in the set defined by this principal reversible square. As these three integers are integral multiples of n, there will always be at least two occurrences of 0 in the unit auxiliary square from which any of these most-perfect squares is composed.

Consequently, there are always at least two occurrences of 0 in one row (or possibly more than one) of one or other of the auxiliary squares of every most-perfect square with $n > 4$.

Appendix C
Methods for constructing pandiagonal magic squares

Pandiagonal magic squares have been made occasionally over many centuries, but their special property of being magic, not only in their rows, columns and principal diagonals, but also in their broken diagonals does not appear to have been noted until Leonhard Euler (1705–1783) defined them. In his endeavours to find a solution to the six officers problem, Euler constructed semi-magic squares (magic in rows and columns but not in diagonals) using pairs of orthogonal Latin squares as auxiliary squares (Section 1.3.1). Multiplying one Latin square, the radix auxiliary, by n, the order of the square, and adding it to the other square, the unit auxiliary, always results in a square that is semi-magic. Euler noted that when the auxiliary squares are appropriately chosen, the resulting square is also magic in all its diagonals, i.e. the sum of the integers in all diagonals is also constant. Since Euler there have been many attempts to construct, but only a very few attempts to enumerate, pandiagonal magic squares. Four of the methods that are, or might have been, pertinent to the construction of most-perfect squares are presented and evaluated here. These four methods are:

(i) the method of paths, due to Frost (1878);
(ii) the method of mixed auxiliary squares with knight's paths, due to Bellew (1997);
(iii) the method of primitive squares, due to Rosser and Walker (1939);
(iv) McClintock's (1897) method for constructing most-perfect squares.

Each method is applied to the construction of squares of order $n = 4$ and $n = 8$; the results are used in Section 1.5. For the first two methods, a procedure is provided for testing whether or not any particular pandiagonal square could have been constructed by that method. These tests are used in Chapter 8.

[115]

C.1 Frost's method of paths

Frost (1878) provided a method for constructing pairs of orthogonal auxiliary squares whose sum, after one square has been multiplied by n, is always a **pandiagonal** magic square (Section 1.2). The method is completely specified only when n is prime. It is based on the fact that, when n is prime, none of the paths $(1, 0)$, $(0, 1)$, $(1, 1)$, $(1, 2)$, ..., $(1, n - 1)$ through any one position in a square, e.g. $(0, 0)$, intersect at any other position. Such paths are then called 'non-intersecting', even though they intersect in their arbitrary starting point.

C.1.1 Construction when n is a prime > 3

When n is a prime > 3, Frost's method of construction is to:

(i) Select two paths from the set of NORMAL PATHS: $(1, 2)$, $(1, 3)$, ..., $(1, n - 2)$. Assign one path, say $(1, r)$, to the radix auxiliary square, and the other path, say $(1, u)$, to the unit auxiliary square.

(ii) Construct the **radix** auxiliary square from n copies of the integers 0 to $(n - 1)$ as follows:

(*a*) place one copy of each integer in any order along the path $(1, u)$ starting at the position $(0, 0)$;

(*b*) place the remaining $(n - 1)$ copies of each integer so that all copies lie along a path $(1, r)$ starting at the position at which the first copy was placed at step (ii)(*a*).

(iii) Construct the **unit** auxiliary square in the same manner, i.e.:

(*a*) place one copy of each integer in any order along the path $(1, r)$ starting at the position $(0, 0)$;

(*b*) place the remaining $(n - 1)$ copies of each integer so that they all lie along a path $(1, u)$.

(iv) Add n times the radix auxiliary to the unit auxiliary square to create the pandiagonal magic square.

An example with $n = 7$ is given in Figure C.1.1, with integers written to the base 7. The paths that have been chosen are $(1, 4)$ for the radix auxiliary and $(1, 3)$ for the unit auxiliary square. The integers chosen for both auxiliary squares are arranged in the order 0 4 1 5 2 6 3. Figure C.1.1*b* shows the radix auxiliary square in the process of construction after one copy of each integer has been placed along the path $(1, u)$ and the integers 0 and 4 have been copied using the path $(1, r)$.

The proof of this method depends upon the paths being non-intersecting when n is prime. In particular in both auxiliary squares the paths $(0, 1)$, $(1, 0)$, $(1, 1)$, $(1, n - 1)$ must each have one copy of each of the n integers 0 to $(n - 1)$. Hence both auxiliary squares are pandiagonal (but not magic, as

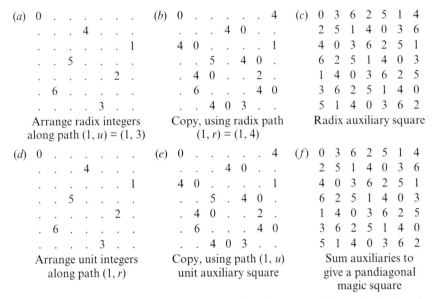

Figure C.1.1 Constructing a 7 by 7 pandiagonal magic square, using paths (1, 4) and (1, 3), by the method of paths (integers written to the base 7).

there are n copies of each integer) and so their sum is also pandiagonal. As the paths do not intersect, the two auxiliary squares are orthogonal, so when they are summed each of the integers 0 to $(n^2 - 1)$ occurs just once. Therefore the matrix sum of n times the radix auxiliary square with the unit auxiliary square is a pandiagonal magic square.

The number of essentially different pandiagonal magic squares that can be generated by this method when n is prime is therefore the number of ways of selecting two of the $(n - 3)$ different normal paths and of arranging the n integers along each path, divided by 8 to avoid double counting of squares that only differ by reflections about three axes, i.e. $(n - 3)(n - 4)(n!)^2 / 8$. Note that for n a prime > 5, there are more pandiagonal magic squares than can be generated by this method (see C.3.3).

C.1.2 Construction when n is not a prime

When n is not prime there are more paths, over and above the normal paths used when n is prime, that can be used for constructing the auxiliary squares. These additional paths are of the form $(r, \pm 1)$. Some of the paths intersect more than once. The choice of the pair of paths used for constructing the auxiliary squares is limited to non-intersecting paths.

The rows, columns and both diagonals are also paths, i.e. (0, 1), (1, 0) and (1, 1) and (1, $n - 1$) respectively. As paths can intersect when n is not prime, the paths chosen for the auxiliary squares may have more than one inter-section with some rows, columns or diagonals (and none with others). Consequently the integers are first arranged in groups, the number of integers in each group being the same as the maximum number of intersections of the chosen paths with a row, column or diagonal. When the integers are placed along a path (see steps (ii)(a) and (iii)(a) of the procedure in Section C.1.1), all integers in one group must be placed in the same row, column or diagonal. For example, when n is doubly-even but not a multiple of 3 or 5, e.g. 4, 8, 16, ..., but not 12, 20, 24, ..., the integers may need to be divided into two groups having the same sum. Frost (1878) gives one ordering of the integers along a path that achieves this: 0, 1, 2, ..., ($\frac{1}{2}n$ − 1), (n − 1), (n − 2), ..., $\frac{1}{2}n$. However, he provides no systematic way of extending the set of paths beyond the normal paths, nor of choosing pairs of non-intersecting paths, nor of arranging the integers into equal-sum groups.

C.1.3 Construction for n = 4

When n = 4 there is only one normal path available to generate both auxiliary squares, namely (1, 2). However, path (2, 1) may also be used. Both paths miss alternate columns/rows and have two integers in the other two columns/rows. Therefore, the integers 0, 1, 2 and 3 must be arranged in two groups of two integers so that the sums within the two groups are equal. There is only one such grouping: 0 with 3 and 1 with 2. Both assignments of paths to the auxiliary squares lead to pandiagonal magic squares that are not essentially different, as shown in Figure C.1.3. Note that this is only one of the three sets of essentially different 4 by 4 pandiagonal magic squares (Figure 1.3.4).

C.1.4 Construction for n = 8

When n = 8, besides the five normal paths there are three additional paths: (2, 1), (4, 1) and (6, 1). (Note that paths (3, 1) and (5, 1) are the same as (1, 3) and (1, 5), respectively, and so need not be added.) The following groups of paths intersect more than once: (1, 2), (1, 4) and (1, 6); (2, 1), (4, 1) and (6, 1), so only one of the two paths can be chosen from each of these groups. There are two other paths that can be freely chosen: (1, 3) and (1, 5).[*] As paths (1, 3) and (1, 5) are non-intersecting, the integers 0 to 7 can be assigned in any order when these paths are chosen. Paths (1, 4) and (4, 1) intersect two of the columns/rows four times and the other six not at all, so if these paths are chosen then the eight integers have to be assigned to two groups, each containing four integers, in such a manner that each group of

---

[*] Frost does not enumerate, but notice that the total number of permissible squares when n = 8 is $(3 \times 3) + (2 \times 6) + 2$ = 23.

(a)
```
0 3 0 3
1 2 1 2
3 0 3 0
2 1 2 1

0 1 3 2
3 2 0 1
0 1 3 2
3 2 0 1
```
Radix
auxiliary
square

(b)
```
0 1 3 2
3 2 0 1
0 1 3 2
3 2 0 1

0 3 0 3
1 2 1 2
3 0 3 0
2 1 2 1
```
Unit
auxiliary
square

(c)
```
00 31 03 32
13 22 10 21
30 01 33 02
23 12 20 11

00 13 30 23
31 22 01 12
03 10 33 20
32 21 02 11
```
Pandiagonal
to the base 4

(d)
```
0  13 3  14
7  10 4  9
12 1  15 2
11 6  8  5

0  7  12 11
13 10 1  6
3  4  15 8
14 9  2  5
```
Pandiagonal
in decimal

Figure C.1.3 The only set of pandiagonal magic squares for $n = 4$, by Frost's method.

integers has the same sum. There are four possibilities for doing this: (0 1 6 7) and (2 3 4 5); (0 2 5 7) and (1 3 4 6); (0 3 5 6) and (1 2 4 7); (0 3 4 7) and (1 2 5 6). The remaining paths intersect four columns or rows twice and so the integers then have to be grouped into four groups of two integers, having equal sums; there is just one way of doing this: (0 7), (1 6), (2 5) and (3 4).

C.1.5 Testing

To test whether a pandiagonal magic square could have been constructed by using the method of paths, first write the integers to the base n. From this construct the unit and radix auxiliary squares. The integers in each auxiliary square must occur in paths. Also the path for integers in the unit auxiliary square, but starting at the position $(0, 0)$ in the **radix** auxiliary square must contain one copy of each of the integers 0 to $(n - 1)$, and vice versa.

C.2 Bellew's method of mixed auxiliary squares

Bellew (1997) uses a pair of orthogonal auxiliary squares, as in Euler's method (Section 1.2), but these auxiliary squares do not each contain integers from 0 to $(n - 1)$. Instead these 'mixed' auxiliary squares contain a selection of integers from 0 to $(n^2 - n)$,[*] in equal-sized runs of equal-spaced integers. (The spacing can be 1, giving consecutive integers.) The two auxiliary squares are then simply added together (without one of them being first multiplied by n) to give a pandiagonal magic square. Each auxiliary square is constructed by using a chess knight's path.

---

[*] The smallest possible largest integer in the 'lower' auxiliary is $(n - 1)$. The largest value for the sum of two integers, one from each auxiliary square, is $(n^2 - 1)$. So the largest possible largest integer in the 'upper' auxiliary will be $(n^2 - 1) - (n - 1) = (n^2 - n)$.

C.2.1 Construction

The method of construction begins by assigning n integers, selected from the range $0 \ldots (n^2 - n)$, to two auxiliary squares, the 'upper' and the 'lower' MIXED AUXILIARY SQUARES. The integer 0 is always assigned to both auxiliary squares, but no other integer may be assigned twice. The integer 1 is always assigned to the LOWER AUXILIARY SQUARE, and it is this that distinguishes the two auxiliary squares. The assignment has to be made in such a way that by summing any pair of integers, one from each auxiliary square, every value from 0 to $(n^2 - 1)$ is arrived at once and only once. Bellew (1997) gives no systematic method for making these assignments. In practice, in correct assignments, the integers come in sequences, in a manner that is similar to the different arrangements of integers in the top row of a reversible square, when using progressive factors (Section 4.4.4).

Next it may be necessary, depending on the factors of n, to arrange the integers assigned to each auxiliary square into equal-sized groups, with the sum of the integers in each group being the same. For example, when n is even and not a multiple of 3, two groups are required. The reason is that then all four knight's paths through $(0, 0)$ pass also through either $(0, \frac{1}{2}n)$ or $(\frac{1}{2}n, 0)$. Hence, an integer assigned to the lower auxiliary square will be at either $(0, \frac{1}{2}n)$ or $(\frac{1}{2}n, 0)$, i.e. in the same row or column as 0. Similarly, two integers assigned to the lower auxiliary will be placed in all rows (or columns). Hence each row (or column) of the lower auxiliary square will consist of two copies of half of the integers assigned to that square. The other half of the integers will appear, twice, in the alternate rows (or columns). Consequently, the integers assigned to the lower auxiliary square must be placed in two equal-size groups having the same sum. The same is true for the integers assigned to the upper auxiliary square. Bellew does not give a general method for doing this.

There are four knight's paths: $(1, \pm 2)$ and $(2, \pm 1)$. Two knight's paths that intersect only at the position $(0,0)$ are chosen, one for the lower and the other for the upper auxiliary square. If none of the paths intersect (except at $(0, 0)$), then there are $4 \times 3 = 12$ possible combinations of pairs of paths that can be assigned to the lower and upper auxiliary squares. Whether or not knight's paths intersect (other than at $(0, 0)$) depends on whether or not 2, 3 or 5 are factors of n:

(i) If 2 is a factor of n, then $\frac{1}{2}n$ steps from $(0, 0)$ along the path $(1, 2)$ is at $(\frac{1}{2}n, n)$, i.e. $(\frac{1}{2}n, 0)$, which is the same as $(\frac{1}{2}n, -n)$, which is $\frac{1}{2}n$ steps from $(0, 0)$ along the path $(1, -2)$. Similarly $\frac{1}{2}n$ steps along the path $(2, 1)$ is also $\frac{1}{2}n$ steps along the path $(2,-1)$.

(ii) If 3 is a factor of n, then $\frac{2}{3}n$ steps along the paths $(1, \pm 2)$ are at $(\frac{2}{3}n, \pm\frac{4}{3}n)$, which are the same positions as $(\frac{2}{3}n, \pm\frac{1}{3}n)$, i.e. $\frac{1}{3}n$ steps along the paths $(2, \pm 1)$, respectively.

(iii) If 5 is a factor of n, then $\frac{2}{5}n$ steps along the paths $(1, \pm 2)$ are at $(\frac{2}{5}n, \pm\frac{4}{5}n)$, which are the same positions as $(\frac{2}{5}n, \mp\frac{1}{5}n)$, i.e. $\frac{1}{5}n$ steps along the paths $(2, \mp 1)$, respectively.

Consequently, if just one of 2, 3 or 5 is a factor of n, then there are $4 \times 2 = 8$ pairs of non-intersecting knight's paths. If any two of 2, 3 or 5 are factors of n, then there are only 4 permissible pairs, i.e. choosing the knight's path for one auxiliary square determines uniquely the knight's path for the other auxiliary square. If 2, 3 and 5 are all factors of n, i.e. n is an integral multiple of 30, then there are no non-intersecting pairs of knight's paths and the method of mixed auxiliary squares produces no pandiagonal magic squares.

The method for constructing a pandiagonal magic square is:

(i) Construct the upper auxiliary square by:

    (*a*) placing the integers assigned to the upper auxiliary square, in some order, along the knight's path for the lower auxiliary square that passes through (0, 0). If these integers have to be arranged in groups, then this is a restriction that now applies. For example, if the integers must be in two equal-sum groups, then the integers from one group must alternate with integers from the other group along the path.

    (*b*) placing the remaining $(n - 1)$ copies of each integer along the upper auxiliary square's knight's path passing through the first copy placed at the previous step, to complete the upper auxiliary square.

(ii) Construct the lower auxiliary square by a process similar to (i) above.

(iii) Sum the integers at the same position in each auxiliary square to give the pandiagonal magic square.

Bellew gives an enumeration of the squares that can be constructed, but only for a few examples, not for the general case.[*]

C.2.2   Construction for $n = 8$

As an illustration, there are ten possible assignments of integers to the upper and lower auxiliary squares when $n = 8$, as shown in octal in Table C.2.2.

There are four possible ways of grouping the integers. For example, the last set of integers assigned to the lower and upper auxiliary squares in Table C.2.2 can be put into two equal-sum groups in the following four ways:

Lower auxiliary square:	Upper auxiliary square:
0 1 60 61; 20 21 40 41	0 2 14 16; 10 12 4 6
0 20 41 61; 1 21 40 60	0 12 4 16; 10 2 14 6
0 21 40 61; 1 20 41 60	0 12 14 6; 10 2 4 16
0 21 41 60; 1 20 40 61	0 10 6 16; 2 12 4 14

[*] A clear enumeration for Bellew's method will appear in D.S. Brée and K. Ollerenshaw, *Pandiagonal magic squares constructed from mixed auxiliary squares.*

Table C.2.2 All ten possible assignments of integers (in octal) to 8 by 8 auxiliary squares

To lower auxiliary square:								To upper auxiliary square:							
0	1	2	3	4	5	6	7	0	10	20	30	40	50	60	70
0	1	2	3	10	11	12	13	0	4	20	24	40	44	60	64
0	1	2	3	20	21	22	23	0	4	10	14	40	44	50	54
0	1	2	3	40	41	42	43	0	4	10	14	20	24	30	34
0	1	4	5	10	11	14	15	0	2	20	22	40	42	60	62
0	1	4	5	20	21	24	25	0	2	10	12	40	42	50	52
0	1	4	5	40	41	44	45	0	2	10	12	20	22	30	32
0	1	10	11	20	21	30	31	0	2	4	6	40	42	44	46
0	1	10	11	40	41	50	51	0	2	4	6	20	22	24	26
0	1	20	21	40	41	60	61	0	2	4	6	10	12	14	16

One of the permitted placings of the last grouping of integers (in octal) for the lower auxiliary square above, along a (2, 1) path assigned to the upper auxiliary square, is shown in Figure C.2.2a. The lower auxiliary square, partly completed by using the path (1, 2), is shown in Figure C.2.2b. Note that although there are two copies of half of the integers in each column, the integers in each column still all have the same sum.

	(a) 0	.	.	.	41	.	.	.		(b) 0	.	21	.	41	.	60	20
		.	.	.	.	.	.	.		60	.	0	.	21	.	41	1
	.	1	.	.	.	40	.	.		41	1	60	.	0	40	21	61
		.	.	.	.	.	.	.		21	.	41	.	60	.	0	40
	.	.	21	.	.	.	60	.		0	.	21	.	41	.	60	20
		.	.	.	.	.	.	.		60	.	0	.	21	.	41	1
	.	.	.	20	.	.	.	61		41	.	60	20	0	.	21	61
		.	.	.	.	.	.	.		21	.	41	.	60	.	0	40

Integers of lower auxiliary square on the path (2, 1) of upper auxiliary

Lower auxiliary square, partly completed by using path (1, 2)

Figure C.2.2 Using both paths, and the (octal) integers assigned to the lower auxiliary square, to construct a lower auxiliary square for $n = 8$.

C.2.3 Test

To recognize whether or not a pandiagonal magic square can be constructed using the method of mixed auxiliary squares, find, if possible, the integers assigned to the two auxiliary squares. As the auxiliary squares are not directly available, they must first be recovered by the following process:

(i) Note that 0 and 1 are always in the lower auxiliary square, so they must always be on the knight's path for the upper auxiliary. If they are not on a. knight's path in the original pandiagonal magic square, this square cannot be constructed by the method of mixed auxiliary squares.

(ii) If 0 and 1 are on a knight's path in the original pandiagonal magic square, the integers along this path are the integers assigned to the lower auxiliary square.

(iii) Test whether these integers come in runs of consecutive integers, each run consisting of the same number of integers. For example, with $n = 8$ the integers (0 1 10 11 40 41 50 51) are arranged in runs of equal length (two), but (0 1 2 10 11 12 40 41) and (0 1 10 11 41 42 50 51) are not. If they are not arranged in equal-length runs, the original square cannot be constructed by the method of mixed auxiliary squares.

(iv) If the integers on this knight's path in the pandiagonal magic square are in equal-length runs, the integers that are needed for the upper auxiliary square can be recovered, as in the construction step. For example, with $n = 8$, if the integers (0 1 10 11 40 41 50 51) are on a knight's path then the integers that are assigned to the upper auxiliary square must be (0 2 4 6 20 22 24 26).

(v) If these integers for the upper auxiliary square do not lie on a second knight's path through the position occupied by 0 in the pandiagonal magic square, the pandiagonal magic square cannot be constructed by this method.

(vi) If these integers do lie on a second knight's path, this is the knight's path for the lower auxiliary square.

(vii) The lower auxiliary square can now be constructed by placing $(n - 1)$ copies of the integers found along the first knight's path (through 0 and 1) along the second knight's path.

(viii) The upper auxiliary square is now found by subtracting the lower auxiliary square from the original pandiagonal magic square.

(ix) If all the copies of the n integers in this upper auxiliary are found along the second knight's path, the original pandiagonal magic square can be constructed by using this method of mixed auxiliary squares; otherwise it cannot.

C.3 Rosser and Walker's primitive squares method

Rosser and Walker (1939) constructed pandiagonal magic squares, not from auxiliary squares but from 'primitive' squares. A PRIMITIVE SQUARE is a square in which the integers in the four corners of any array within the square have equal cross sums. Primitive squares come in sets, with one 'normalized primitive square' in each set. A NORMALIZED PRIMITIVE SQUARE is a primitive square with 0 at (0, 0), with 1 at (0, 1) and the integers in every row or every column in ascending order.

C.3.1 Primitive squares

If any two rows or columns of a primitive square are exchanged, all the arrays will still have equal cross sums, so the resulting square is still primitive. Hence, the rows and columns of any primitive square can be exchanged to reach a primitive square with 0 at (0, 0) and the integers in the top row and left column in ascending order. If 1 is at (1, 0), reflect the square about the downward-sloping principal diagonal (which results in a square that is not essentially different) to bring 1 to the position (0, 1). In this normalized primitive square the integers in all the rows, not just the top row, and in all the columns, not just the left column, will be in ascending order. To show this, let the integers at (i, j) in a primitive square Q be $q_{i,j}$. As all arrays have equal cross sums and the top row and left column are in ascending order:

$$q_{i,j} + q_{g,h} = q_{i,h} + q_{g,j}, \quad \text{for } i \neq g, \ j \neq h,$$

and
$$q_{0,j} < q_{0,j+j'} \quad \text{and} \quad q_{i,0} < q_{i+i',0}$$
$$\text{for all } 0 < i' < (n-i), \ 0 < j' < (n-j).$$

So $\quad q_{i,j} = q_{i,0} + q_{0,j} - q_{0,0} < q_{i+i',0} + q_{0,j+j'} - q_{0,0} = q_{i+i',j+j'}. \quad$ (C.3.1.1)

It is now shown that integers in the rows of a normalized primitive square occur in runs of f consecutive integers. If this is true, it must also be true for the first row by equal cross sums. Assume that this is false for the top row. Let gf integers in the top row occur in such runs, but suppose that

$$q_{0,gf}, \ q_{0,gf+1}, \ \cdots, \ q_{0,(g-1)f-1}$$

are not consecutive integers. Then the integer $(q_{0,gf} + k)$, where $0 < k < f$, is not in the top row. Let it be at (i, j), where $i > 0$. Then:

(i) If $0 \leq j < (gf + k)$, the integer $(q_{0,gf} + k)$ occurs in a run. As the integer $(q_{0,gf} + k - 1)$ is in the top row, the integer $(q_{0,gf} + k)$ cannot occur in the middle of a run, so it would have to be at the beginning of a run, i.e.

$$q_{i,g'f} = q_{0,gf} + k, \quad \text{where } 0 \leq g' < g.$$

Then $\quad q_{i,g'f+f-k} = q_{0,gf} + f, \quad \text{as } 0 < (f-k) < f.$

But $\quad q_{0,0} + q_{1,gf} = q_{1,0} + q_{0,gf} \quad$ by equal cross sums,

and $\quad q_{0,0} = 0 \quad \text{and} \quad q_{1,0} = f.$

Hence $\quad q_{1,gf} = q_{0,gf} + f = q_{i,g'f+f-k} \quad$ by substitution,

which requires that $f = k$, contrary to the assumption. So $j \geq (gf + k)$.

(ii) If $(gf + k) \leq j < n$, the integer $(q_{0,gf} + k)$ would be less than the integer at $q_{0,j}$, which is contrary to (C.3.1.1).

There is therefore no permissible value of j, so the assumption is false. Hence the integers in a primitive square must occur in runs of f consecutive integers.

Similarly the integers in the rows must occur in runs of m integers that are f apart, e.g. $0, f, 2f, ..., (m - 1)f$. Let the rectangle R be made of the integers:

$$r_{i,j} = q_{i,fj}/f, \quad 0 \le i < n, \ 0 \le j < n/f.$$

Then $\qquad\qquad r_{0,0} = 0 \quad$ and $\quad r_{1,0} = 1$

and R is primitive. The above argument holds equally well for rectangles and for squares. Interchanging rows and columns, and applying the same argument again, shows that the integers in the rows of the rectangle must be in multiples of m consecutive integers, i.e. the integers in the columns of the square Q must be in sequences of m integers that are f apart.

This process can be repeated to arrive at another rectangle and so on. Eventually the process will terminate when the sequences are of length one. Note that the number of times this is done for sequences in the columns must always be the same as, or one less than, the number of times it is done for rows.

C.3.2 Construction

To construct a normalized primitive square, choose two sequences of progressive factors of n, such that $1 < f_1 < f_2 < ... < f_u < n$ and $1 < n_1 < n_2 < ... n_v < n$, where f_i is a factor of f_{i+1}, n_i is a factor of n_{i+1} and $u = v$ or $u = v + 1$. Then construct the entire primitive square in the same way as is used for constructing the largest corner block of a reversible square (Section 4.4.4).

The primitive square is then transformed into a pandiagonal magic square using a transform of the form

$$T = \begin{bmatrix} a & c \\ b & d \end{bmatrix},$$

i.e. a square P with elements $p_{ai+cj, bi+dj} = q_{i,j}$. If $abcd\,(a^2 - b^2)(c^2 - d^2)$ is prime to n, then T is a REGULAR TRANSFORM and P is guaranteed to be a pandiagonal magic square.

If n is even then there are no such values of a, b, c and d. (a, b, c and d must be odd to be prime to n, but then $(a^2 - b^2)$ and $(c^2 - d^2)$ are both even and so not prime to n.) Recall that there are no singly-even pandiagonal magic squares. However, there are non-regular transforms that make a primitive square into a pandiagonal magic square for doubly-even n. One such transform is:

$$T = \begin{bmatrix} 2 & -1 \\ -3 & 2 \end{bmatrix}.$$

Rosser and Walker give no method for selecting just those transforms that result in pandiagonal magic squares. Consequently, to find those values of T that do result in pandiagonal magic squares all the values of a, b, c and d between 0 and $(n - 1)$ have to be considered. The search can be restricted because, if either b or d is prime to n, it can be set to 1, as shown by Rosser and Walker.

C.3.3 Enumeration

The number of primitive squares in any set is the number of ways of reordering the rows and columns, i.e. $(n!)^2$. Rosser and Walker (1939) do not give a general formula for $\psi(n)$, the number of normalized primitive squares, i.e. the number of ways of finding pairs of sequences of progressive factors of n. They note simply that $\psi(n) \leq (n!)^2$ and $\psi(p) = 1$, where p is prime (as p has no progressive factors).

The number of regular transforms is given by $\theta(n)$, say, where

(i) $\theta(2^r) = 0$,
(ii) $\theta(p^s) = p^{2s-2}(p - 3)(p - 4)$ if p is an odd prime, and
(iii) $\theta(mn) = \theta(m)\theta(n)$ if m and n have no common factors other than 1.

However, there are other, non-regular, Ts that will transform a primitive square into a pandiagonal magic square. There is no general formula for the number of these non-regular transforms. In addition, Rosser and Walker prove that for all values of n, except 1, 3, 4 and 5 and n modulo 4 = 2, there are pandiagonal magic squares that cannot be reached from any of the primitive squares via any transform of the form T.

C.3.4 Construction and enumeration when $n = 4$

When $n = 4$ there is only one progressive factor between 1 and 4, namely 2. So three normalized primitive squares can be made with the sets of factors for rows and columns: $(-, -)$, $(2, 2)$, $(2, -)$, respectively, where a dash signifies no progressive factor. The top rows and left columns of the primitive squares from these three sets of progressive factors are shown in Table C.3.4. Recall that if either b or d in T is prime to n, i.e. for $n = 8$, that b or d is odd, then it can be set to 1. So the values of T that can transform a primitive square into a pandiagonal magic square are:

b	d	a	c	Number
1	1	$\{0, 1, 2, 3\}$	$\{0, 1, 2, 3\}$	4^2
1	$\{0, 2\}$	$\{0, 1, 2, 3\}$	$\{0, 1, 2, 3\}$	2×4^2
$\{0, 2\}$	1	$\{0, 1, 2, 3\}$	$\{0, 1, 2, 3\}$	2×4^2
$\{0, 2\}$	$\{0, 2\}$	$\{0, 1, 2, 3\}$	$\{0, 1, 2, 3\}$	4×4^2

This places an upper bound of $3 \times 9 \times 4^2 = 432$ possible 4 by 4 pandiagonal magic squares that could be constructed from just the normalized primitive squares. There are only $48 = 432/9$ essentially different pandiagonal magic squares (see the list of all 4 by 4 magic squares given in Ollerenshaw and Bondi, 1982), so not all values of T transform a normalized primitive square into an essentially different pandiagonal magic square.

Table C.3.4 Normalized primitive squares for $n = 4$, with integers written to the base 4

Progressive factors		Normalized primitive squares							
Rows	Columns	Top row				Left column			
–	–	0	1	2	3	0	4	8	12
2	2	0	1	4	5	0	2	8	10
2	–	0	1	8	9	0	2	4	6

C.3.5 Construction and upper bound for $n = 8$

When $n = 8$ there are two progressive factors between 1 and 8, namely $2 < 4$. Ten sets (for rows and columns) of progressive factors can be made, as shown in Table C.3.5. Using these ten sets, ten normalized primitive squares with top rows and left columns as shown, in octal, in Table C.3.5, can be constructed. The values of T that **may** transform a primitive square into a pandiagonal magic square are:

b	d	a	c	Number
1	1	$\{0, ..., 7\}$	$\{0, ..., 7\}$	8^2
1	$\{0, 2, 4\ 6\}$	$\{0, ..., 7\}$	$\{0, ..., 7\}$	4×8^2
$\{0, 2, 4\ 6\}$	1	$\{0, ..., 7\}$	$\{0, ..., 7\}$	4×8^2
$\{0, 2, 4\ 6\}$	$\{0, 2, 4\ 6\}$	$\{0, ..., 7\}$	$\{0, ..., 7\}$	16×8^2

This places an upper bound of $10 \times 25 \times 8^2 = 16,000$ on the number of 8 by 8 pandiagonal squares that it might be possible to construct from normalized primitive squares. There are $(8!)^2/8$ essentially different primitive squares for every normalized primitive square. Hence the upper bound on the number of essentially different pandiagonal magic squares that might be able to be constructed by the method of primitive squares is $2000 \times (8!)^2 = 3.25 \times 10^{12}$.

Moreover, not all 8 by 8 pandiagonal magic squares can be produced in this manner. Rosser and Walker provide an alternative method of construction that generates $192^{(n/4)^2}\left[2\left(\frac{1}{4}n\right)^2\right]!/8$ essentially different pandiagonal magic squares when n is doubly-even. For $n = 8$ this number is $192^4 \times 7! = 6.85 \times 10^{12}$, which is greater than the upper bound on the number of essentially different pandiagonal magic squares that might be able to be constructed from primitive squares.

Table C.3.5 Normalized primitive squares for $n = 8$, with integers written in octal.

Progressive factors		Normalized primitive squares															
Rows	Columns	Top row								Left column							
–	–	0	1	2	3	4	5	6	7	0	10	20	30	40	50	60	70
4	2	0	1	2	3	10	11	12	13	0	4	20	24	40	44	60	64
4	4	0	1	2	3	20	21	22	23	0	4	10	14	40	44	50	54
4	–	0	1	2	3	40	41	42	43	0	4	10	14	20	24	30	34
2	2	0	1	4	5	10	11	14	15	0	2	20	22	40	42	60	62
2, 4	2, 4	0	1	4	5	20	21	24	25	0	2	10	12	40	42	50	52
2, 4	2	0	1	4	5	40	41	44	45	0	2	10	12	20	22	30	32
2	4	0	1	10	11	20	21	30	31	0	2	4	6	40	42	44	46
2, 4	4	0	1	10	11	40	41	50	51	0	2	4	6	20	22	24	26
2	–	0	1	20	21	40	41	60	61	0	2	4	6	10	12	14	16

C.4 McClintock's figure-of-eight method for most-perfect squares

McClintock (1897) developed two methods for constructing pandiagonal magic squares having 'most perfect form', one for squares of odd order and one for doubly-even squares (there are no singly-even pandiagonal magic squares). Consider only the method for doubly-even squares.

C.4.1 The method of construction

The method starts by constructing squares in which:

   (i) alternate rows are similar;

   (ii) all the vertical couplets in a pair of adjacent rows have the same sum;

   (iii) the integers in the bottom half of the square are S-complements of the corresponding integers distant $\frac{1}{2}n$ along a diagonal in the top half of the square ($S = (n^2 - 1)$).

Call these squares McCLINTOCK SQUARES. These McClintock squares can be transformed into most-perfect squares by replacing integers in all the odd (or in all the even) columns by their S-complements.

The construction of McClintock squares involves arranging sequences of consecutive integers in different ways. There is a standard way of doing this, given by McClintock, and variations on the standard, that are not completely specified. The standard way arranges integers in figures-of-eight:

   (i) The first n consecutive integers are placed in the upper two rows with 0 to $(\frac{1}{2}n - 1)$ in the left half of the top row and $\frac{1}{2}n$ to $(n - 1)$ in the right half of the next row, both from left to right.

   (ii) The next n consecutive integers are placed so as to fill up the remaining places in the top two rows: n to $(\frac{3}{2}n - 1)$ in the right half of the top row and to $\frac{3}{2}n$ to $(2n - 1)$ in the left half of the next row, both from right to left.

(iii) This process is repeated, placing the next $2n$ integers in the next pair of rows until the top half of the square is complete.

To convert this top half of a McClintock square into a most-perfect square:

(iv) The integers in the odd (or the even) columns of the half square are replaced by their S-complements, where $S = (n^2 - 1)$.

(v) The bottom half of the square is completed by placing S-complements at a distance of $\frac{1}{2}n$ along the diagonal from all the integers in the top half of the square.

Note that this construction will generate a most-perfect square for any doubly-even n. The process for $n = 8$ is shown, with integers in octal, in Figure C.4.1.

(a)	0	1	2	3	13	12	11	10	(b)	0	76	2	74	13	65	11	67
	17	16	15	14	4	5	6	7		17	61	15	63	4	72	6	70
	20	21	22	23	33	32	31	30		20	56	22	54	33	45	31	47
	37	36	35	34	24	25	26	27		37	41	35	43	24	52	26	50

$$\begin{array}{cccc|cccc}
0 & 76 & 2 & 74 & 13 & 65 & 11 & 67 \\
17 & 61 & 15 & 63 & 4 & 72 & 6 & 70 \\
20 & 56 & 22 & 54 & 33 & 45 & 31 & 47 \\
37 & 41 & 35 & 43 & 24 & 52 & 26 & 50 \\
\hline - & & & & + & & & - \\
64 & 12 & 66 & 10 & 77 & 1 & 75 & 3 \\
73 & 5 & 71 & 7 & 60 & 16 & 62 & 14 \\
44 & 32 & 46 & 30 & 57 & 21 & 55 & 23 \\
53 & 25 & 51 & 27 & 40 & 36 & 42 & 34
\end{array}$$

McClintock square (top half)   Most-perfect square

Figure C.4.1 The standard figure-of-eight construction for $n = 8$, in octal.

The variations on the figure-of-eight method were only illustrated by McClintock, e.g. using just the even numbers in the top left row. They are not completely specified, so the procedure requires trial and error to find the variations. It is, reproduced to the best of our ability, as follows:

(i) Choose the pairs of integers to be placed in the left and right halves of the top two rows as follows:

(a) Choose s, the sum of vertical couplets in the top two rows.

(b) Choose n distinct pairs of integers having this sum.

(c) Select half of these, say the 'left' half, the rest being the 'right' half. The selection must be such that adding a fixed amount, say u_0, to the lower integer of each left pair gives an integer in one of the right pairs.

(ii) Place these integers in the top two rows:

(a) Place the lower integer of the left pairs in the left half of the top row, in ascending order, and the higher integer of each left pair in the next row in the same order.

(b) Arrange the right pairs in the same order as the left pairs, using the matching of step (i)(c). Then place the pairs from left to right, in the right half of the square, with the integer that is u_0 larger in the next row and the other integer in the top row.

(iii) For $i = 2$ to $(\frac{1}{2}n - 2)$, in steps of 2:

    (a) Choose a value v_i. Add v_i to the integers in the left half of the first two rows to give the integers in the left half of the rows i and $(i + 1)$.

    (b) Choose a value u_i. Add u_i to the integers in the left half of rows i and $(i + 1)$ to fill the corresponding columns in the right half of these rows.

This must give the top half of a McClintock square, i.e. a half square in which all the vertical couplets in any pair of adjacent rows have a constant sum, and that no pairs of integers are S-complements because these must be reserved for the bottom half. Consequently the integers must be as shown in Table C.4.1, in which the $q_{0,j}$ and the u_i and v_i have to be chosen.

Table C.4.1 Integers in McClintock squares

Row	Columns, $j = $	$0 \ldots (\frac{1}{2}n - 1)$	$\frac{1}{2}n \ldots (n - 1)$
0		$q_{0,j}$	$s - (q_{0,j} + u_0)$
1		$s - q_{0,j}$	$q_{0,j} + u_0$
i		$v_i + q_{0,j}$	$v_i + s - (q_{0,j} + u_i)$
$i + 1$		$v_i + s - q_{0,j}$	$v_i + q_{0,j} + u_i$

The sum of the integers in a vertical couplet in the left half of rows $(i + 1)$ and $(i + 2)$ is:

$$v_i + s - q_{0,j} + v_{i+2} + q_{0,j} = s + v_i + v_{i+2}.$$

Note that this is independent of j, i.e. it is constant. The sum of vertical couplets in the right half of rows $(i + 1)$ and $(i + 2)$ is:

$$v_i + q_{0,j} + u_i + v_{i+2} + s - (q_{0,j} + u_{i+2}) = s + v_i + v_{i+2} + u_i - u_{i+2},$$

i.e. it is also constant. These two constants must be the same for a McClintock square, so $u_{i+2} = u_i$. This gives a necessary condition on the construction, which was not given by McClintock, namely that all the u_i are the same.

C.4.2 Construction for $n = 4$

As an illustration, the three most-perfect squares that can be constructed when $n = 4$ by using McClintock's squares are shown in Figure C.4.2.

C.4.3 One-to-one correspondence

In McClintock squares the pair of integers in **all** the vertical couplets in any pair of adjacent rows have a constant sum. Because the integers in every odd

	7		11
Select s:	7		11
All possible pairs:	(0, 7) (1, 6) (2, 5) (3, 4)		(0, 11) (1, 10) (2, 9) (3, 8)
Select u:	4	2	2
Choose left group of pairs:	(0, 7) (1, 6)	(0, 7) (1, 6)	(0, 11) (1, 10)
and right group of pairs:	(4, 3) (5, 2)	(2, 5) (3, 4)	(2, 9) (3, 8)

Top half of
   McClintock square:

```
 0  1  3  2     0  1  5  4     0  1  9  8
 7  6  4  5     7  6  2  3    11 10  2  3
```

Replace odd columns
   by S-complements:
And add bottom half:

```
 0 14  3 13     0 14  5 11     0 14  9  7
 7  9  4 10     7  9  2 12    11  5  2 12
12  2 15  1    10  4 15  1     6  8 15  1
11  5  8  6    13  3  8  6    13  3  4 10
```

Figure C.4.2 Constructing 4 by 4 most-perfect squares by using McClintock squares.

column are replaced by their S-complements, the sum of any 2×2 array in the final square is $2S$, i.e. it is constant. As the bottom half of the final square is completed by using S-complements at a distance of $\frac{1}{2}n$ along diagonals, both conditions for a most-perfect square (2.2.1.1, 2.2.1.2) are satisfied, so this method always generates most-perfect squares.

Given any most-perfect square, the integers in the bottom half are always the S-complements of those in the top half. Consider just the top half. Note that the vertical couplets in even columns of a pair of rows have the same sum, as do the vertical couplets in odd columns, and that the sum of these two sums together is $2S$ (2.2.3.1). Replace the integers in the odd columns by their S-complements. The vertical couplets in odd columns will now have the same sum as the adjacent vertical couplets in even columns. So all the vertical couplets in any pair of rows will have a constant sum, i.e. they form the top half of a McClintock square. The bottom half of the square is then completed by using S-complements of the integers in the top half. To do so, place the S-complements at positions that are reflections in the centre point of the square. It follows that McClintock (1897, §21) was correct to believe that his method could generate all most-perfect squares.

C.4.4 Construction for $n = 8$

That the method of using McClintock squares can generate all most-perfect squares was confirmed for $n = 8$ by Ollerenshaw (1986). The method generates the ten sets of squares, as shown in Table C.4.4. Other combinations of s and u give squares that are the same as those already obtained. This repetition renders the method unsuitable for construction and impossible for enumeration for $n > 8$.

If the right and left halves of the odd rows of a McClintock square are interchanged and the right halves of all rows reversed, the result is a reversible square. Applying this transform to the ten McClintock squares in Table C.4.4 produces the principal reversible squares for the ten sets of 8 by

Table C.4.4 The ten sets of McClintock squares for $n = 8$, with integers in octal

s	Eight pairs	u	Left and right groups	Top two rows							
17	(0,17) ... (7,10)	10	(0,17)(1,16)(2,15)(3,14)	0	1	2	3	7	6	5	4
			(10,7)(11,6)(12,5)(13,4)	17	16	15	14	10	11	12	13
		4	(0,17)(1,16)(2,15)(3,14)	0	1	2	3	13	12	11	10
			(4,13)(5,12)(6,11)(7,10)	17	16	15	14	4	5	6	7
		2	(0,17)(1,16)(4,13)(5,12)	0	1	4	5	15	14	11	10
			(2,15)(3,14)(6,11)(7,10)	17	16	13	12	2	3	6	7
27	(0,27) ... (7,20)	4	(0,27)(1,26)(2,25)(3,24)	0	1	2	3	23	22	21	20
			(4,23)(5,22)(6,21)(7,20)	27	26	25	24	4	5	6	7
		2	(0,27)(1,26)(4,23)(5,22)	0	1	4	5	25	24	21	20
			(2,25)(3,24)(6,21)(7,20)	27	26	23	22	2	3	6	7
47	(0,47) ... (7,40)	4	(0,47)(1,46)(2,45)(3,44)	0	1	2	3	43	42	41	40
			(4,43)(5,42)(6,41)(7,40)	47	46	45	44	4	5	6	7
		2	(0,47)(1,46)(4,43)(5,42)	0	1	4	5	45	44	41	40
			(2,45)(3,44)(6,41)(7,40)	47	46	43	42	2	3	6	7
33	(0,33) ... (3,30)	2	(0,33)(1,32)(10,23)(11,22)	0	1	10	11	31	30	21	20
	(10,23) ... (13,20)		(2,31)(3,30)(12,21)(13,20)	33	32	23	22	2	3	12	13
53	(0,53) ... (3,50)	2	(0,53)(1,52)(10,43)(11,42)	0	1	10	11	51	50	41	40
	(10,43) ... (13,40)		(2,51)(3,50)(12,41)(13,40)	53	52	43	42	2	3	12	13
63	(0,63) ... (3,60)	2	(0,63)(1,62)(20,43)(21,42)	0	1	20	21	61	60	41	40
	(20,43) ... (23,40)		(2,61)(3,60)(22,41)(23,40)	63	62	43	42	2	3	22	23

8 most-perfect squares. This can be confirmed by comparing the top rows of the ten McClintock squares with the top rows of the ten normalized primitive squares in Table C.3.5. (Recall that normalized primitive squares are equivalent to principal reversible squares.)

This method provides another way of transforming reversible squares to most-perfect squares: first transform the reversible square into a McClintock square and then the McClintock square into a most-perfect square. It can be shown that there is a one-to-one correspondence between reversible squares and McClintock squares. Therefore, the one-to-one correspondence between reversible squares and most-perfect squares, established in Chapter 3 by using the transform T on primitive squares, is confirmed.

Appendix D

Construction of most-perfect squares from reversible squares

To construct a most-perfect square from a reversible square:

(i) Construct a principal reversible square, R, with elements $r_{i,j}$. The algorithm for doing this is given in Figure D.1.

(ii) Transform the principal reversible square into any reversible square, R' (with elements $r'_{i,j}$), in the same set, by interchanging complementary pairs of rows/columns (2.4.1.5, 2.4.1.6) or by interchanging pairs of rows/columns in one half of the square and, at the same time, interchanging the pair of rows/columns in the other half of the square that are complementary to the first pair (2.4.1.7, 2.4.1.8).

(iii) As shown in Section 3.1.1, reverse the right half of each row and the bottom half of each column of reversible square R' to give the intermediary square Q, with elements:

$$q_{i,j} = \begin{cases} r'_{i,j} & \text{for } i < k, \ j < k; \\ r'_{i,\,3k-1-j} & \text{for } i < k, \ j \geq k; \\ r'_{3k-1-i,\,j} & \text{for } i \geq k, \ j < k; \\ r'_{3k-1-i,\,3k-1-j} & \text{for } i \geq k, \ j \geq k. \end{cases}$$

Then apply to Q the transform:

$$T = \begin{bmatrix} 1 & \frac{1}{2}n \\ \frac{1}{2}n & \frac{1}{2}n + 1 \end{bmatrix}.$$

The result of applying T to Q is a most-perfect square P, with elements:

$$p_{i,j} = q_{i+\frac{1}{2}nj,\,\frac{1}{2}ni+(\frac{1}{2}n+1)j} = q_{i+\frac{1}{2}jn,\,j+\frac{1}{2}(i+j)n}.$$

Given $n = \prod_{0 \le g \le G} p_g^{s_g}$, with p_g different primes, $p_0 = 2$; s_g an integer > 0, $s_0 \ge 2$.
To construct a principal reversible square, R, with elements $r_{i,j}$:

(i) Choose a set of indices $\{s'_0, \dots, s'_G\}$ such that $0 \le s'_g \le s_g$ and $\sum_{0 \le g \le G} s'_g > 0$.
                                                     % for the progressive factors f_h
     Let $f = \prod_{0 \le g \le G} p_g^{s'_g}$.   % f is the width of the largest corner block

(ii) Choose a value of v such that $0 \le v < \sum_{0 \le g \le G} s'_g$.
                                          % v is the number of progressive factors

(iii) For $g = 0$ up to G, let $s''_g = s_g$.   % for the values of the progressive factors n_h

(iv) Let $f_{v+1} = f$ and $n_{v+1} = n$.   % $n \times f$ is size of largest corner block

(v) For $h = v$ down to 1:   % Select the v progressive factors of f and n
     • decrease one or more values of s'_g, $0 \le g \le G$,
       subject to the constraint $\sum_{0 \le g \le G} s'_g \ge h$;
     • let $f_h = \prod_{0 \le g \le G} p_g^{s'_g}$;   % f_h is the hth progressive factor of f
     • decrease one or more values of s''_g, $0 \le g \le G$,
       subject to the constraint $\sum_{0 \le g \le G} s''_g \ge h$;
     • let $n_h = \prod_{0 \le g \le G} p_g^{s''_g}$.   % n_h is the hth progressive factor of n

(vi) For $i = 0$ up to n_1:
     • for $j = 0$ up to f_1:   % size of smallest corner block
     • let $r_{i,j} = if_1 + j$.   % create the smallest corner block

(vii) For $h = 1$ up to v: % for all pairs of progressive factors f_h, n_h
     • for $I = 0$ up to $(n_{h+1}/n_h - 1)$:   % number of layers of copies
     • for $J = 0$ up to $(f_{h+1}/f_h - 1)$:   % number of copies in each layer
     • let shift $= (If_{h+1} + Jf_h)n_h$ % shift is amount added for this copy
     • for $i = 0$ up to $(n_h - 1)$:
       • for $j = 0$ up to $(f_h - 1)$:   % size of corner block
       • let $r_{In_h+i,\, Jf_h+j} = $ shift $+ r_{i,j}$.   % copy the corner block
                                  % The largest corner block is now complete.

(viii) For $J = 1$ up to $n/f - 1$:   % number of copies of largest corner block
     • let shift $= Jfn$ % shift is the amount to be added for this copy
     • for $i = 0$ up to $(n - 1)$:
       • for $j = 0$ up to $(f - 1)$:   % size of largest corner block
       • let $r_{i,\, Jf+j} = $ shift $+ r_{i,j}$.   % copy the largest corner block
                            % The principal reversible square is now complete.

Figure D.1 Algorithm for the construction of a principal reversible square.

Appendix E

Complete list of principal reversible squares of order 12

In this appendix are listed all the 42 principal reversible squares of order $n = 12$. They are presented in three groups, according to the number of progressive factors chosen to make the largest corner block: none, one or two. Within each grouping, the squares are arranged by f, the factor of n chosen as the width of the largest corner block, and by the progressive factor(s) of f, where these exist.

E.1 No progressive factors

The smallest corner block is also the largest corner block.

```
 0  1   24 25   48 49 | 72 73    96  97   120 121
 2  3   26 27   50 51   74 75    98  99   122 123
 4  5   28 29   52 53   76 77   100 101   124 125
 6  7   30 31   54 55   78 79   102 103   126 127
 8  9   32 33   56 57   80 81   104 105   128 129
10 11   34 35   58 59   82 83   106 107   130 131
12 13   36 37   60 61   84 85   108 109   132 133
14 15   38 39   62 63   86 87   110 111   134 135
16 17   40 41   64 65   88 89   112 113   136 137
18 19   42 43   66 67   90 91   114 115   138 139
20 21   44 45   68 69   92 93   116 117   140 141
22 23   46 47   70 71 | 94 95   118 119   142 143
                f = 2
```

```
 0  1  2  3   48 49|50 51   96  97  98  99
 4  5  6  7   52 53 54 55  100 101 102 103
 8  9 10 11   56 57 58 59  104 105 106 107
12 13 14 15   60 61 62 63  108 109 110 111
16 17 18 19   64 65 66 67  112 113 114 115
20 21 22 23   68 69 70 71  116 117 118 119
24 25 26 27   72 73 74 75  120 121 122 123
28 29 30 31   76 77 78 79  124 125 126 127
32 33 34 35   80 81 82 83  128 129 130 131
36 37 38 39   84 85 86 87  132 133 134 135
40 41 42 43   88 89 90 91  136 137 138 139
44 45 46 47   92 93|94 95  140 141 142 143
                f = 4
```

```
 0  1  2   36 37 38 | 72  73  74   108 109 110
 3  4  5   39 40 41   75  76  77   111 112 113
 6  7  8   42 43 44   78  79  80   114 115 116
 9 10 11   45 46 47   81  82  83   117 118 119
12 13 14   48 49 50   84  85  86   120 121 122
15 16 17   51 52 53   87  88  89   123 124 125
18 19 20   54 55 56   90  91  92   126 127 128
21 22 23   57 58 59   93  94  95   129 130 131
24 25 26   60 61 62   96  97  98   132 133 134
27 28 29   63 64 65   99 100 101   135 136 137
30 31 32   66 67 68  102 103 104   138 139 140
33 34 35   69 70 71 | 105 106 107  141 142 143
                f = 3
```

```
 0  1  2  3  4  5 | 72  73  74  75  76  77
 6  7  8  9 10 11   78  79  80  81  82  83
12 13 14 15 16 17   84  85  86  87  88  89
18 19 20 21 22 23   90  91  92  93  94  95
24 25 26 27 28 29   96  97  98  99 100 101
30 31 32 33 34 35  102 103 104 105 106 107
36 37 38 39 40 41  108 109 110 111 112 113
42 43 44 45 46 47  114 115 116 117 118 119
48 49 50 51 52 53  120 121 122 123 124 125
54 55 56 57 58 59  126 127 128 129 130 131
60 61 62 63 64 65  132 133 134 135 136 137
66 67 68 69 70 71 | 138 139 140 141 142 143
                f = 6
```

```
  0   1   2   3   4   5 | 6   7   8   9  10  11
 12  13  14  15  16  17  18  19  20  21  22  23
 24  25  26  27  28  29  30  31  32  33  34  35
 36  37  38  39  40  41  42  43  44  45  46  47
 48  49  50  51  52  53  54  55  56  57  58  59
 60  61  62  63  64  65  66  67  68  69  70  71
 72  73  74  75  76  77  78  79  80  81  82  83
 84  85  86  87  88  89  90  91  92  93  94  95
 96  97  98  99 100 101 102 103 104 105 106 107
108 109 110 111 112 113 114 115 116 117 118 119
120 121 122 123 124 125 126 127 128 129 130 131
132 133 134 135 136 137|138 139 140 141 142 143
                f = 12
```

E.2   One progressive factor

E.2.1 $f_1 = 2$, $f = 4$

```
 0  1    4  5    48 49| 52 53    96  97    100 101
 2  3    6  7    50 51  54 55    98  99    102 103

 8  9   12 13    56 57  60 61    104 105   108 109
10 11   14 15    58 59  62 63    106 107   110 111

16 17   20 21    64 65  68 69    112 113   116 117
18 19   22 23    66 67  70 71    114 115   118 119

24 25   28 29    72 73  76 77    120 121   124 125
26 27   30 31    74 75  78 79    122 123   126 127

32 33   36 37    80 81  84 85    128 129   132 133
34 35   38 39    82 83  86 87    130 131   134 135

40 41   44 45    88 89  92 93    136 137   140 141
42 43   46 47    90 91| 94 95    138 139   142 143

                  n₁ = 2
```

```
 0  1    8  9    48 49| 56 57    96  97    104 105
 2  3   10 11    50 51  58 59    98  99    106 107

 4  5   12 13    52 53  60 61    100 101   108 109
 6  7   14 15    54 55  62 63    102 103   110 111

16 17   24 25    64 65  72 73    112 113   120 121
18 19   26 27    66 67  74 75    114 115   122 123

20 21   28 29    68 69  76 77    116 117   124 125
22 23   30 31    70 71  78 79    118 119   126 127

32 33   40 41    80 81  88 89    128 129   136 137
34 35   42 43    82 83  90 91    130 131   138 139

36 37   44 45    84 85  92 93    132 133   140 141
38 39   46 47    86 87| 94 95    134 135   142 143

                  n₁ = 4
```

```
 0  1    6  7    48 49| 54 55    96  97    102 103
 2  3    8  9    50 51  56 57    98  99    104 105
 4  5   10 11    52 53  58 59    100 101   106 107

12 13   18 19    60 61  66 67    108 109   114 115
14 15   20 21    62 63  68 69    110 111   116 117
16 17   22 23    64 65  70 71    112 113   118 119

24 25   30 31    72 73  78 79    120 121   126 127
26 27   32 33    74 75  80 81    122 123   128 129
28 29   34 35    76 77  82 83    124 125   130 131

36 37   42 43    84 85  90 91    132 133   138 139
38 39   44 45    86 87  92 93    134 135   140 141
40 41   46 47    88 89| 94 95    136 137   142 143

                  n₁ = 3
```

```
 0  1   12 13    48 49| 60 61    96  97    108 109
 2  3   14 15    50 51  62 63    98  99    110 111
 4  5   16 17    52 53  64 65    100 101   112 113
 6  7   18 19    54 55  66 67    102 103   114 115
 8  9   20 21    56 57  68 69    104 105   116 117
10 11   22 23    58 59  70 71    106 107   118 119

24 25   36 37    72 73  84 85    120 121   132 133
26 27   38 39    74 75  86 87    122 123   134 135
28 29   40 41    76 77  88 89    124 125   136 137
30 31   42 43    78 79  90 91    126 127   138 139
32 33   44 45    80 81  92 93    128 129   140 141
34 35   46 47    82 83| 94 95    130 131   142 143

                  n₁ = 6
```

E.2.2 $f_1 = 2,\ f = 6$

```
 0  1    4  5    8  9  | 72  73   76  77   80  81
 2  3    6  7   10 11    74  75   78  79   82  83
12 13   16 17   20 21    84  85   88  89   92  93
14 15   18 19   22 23    86  87   90  91   94  95
24 25   28 29   32 33    96  97  100 101  104 105
26 27   30 31   34 35    98  99  102 103  106 107
36 37   40 41   44 45 + 108 109  112 113  116 117
38 39   42 43   46 47   110 111  114 115  118 119
48 49   52 53   56 57   120 121  124 125  128 129
50 51   54 55   58 59   122 123  126 127  130 131
60 61   64 65   68 69   132 133  136 137  140 141
62 63   66 67   70 71 | 134 135  138 139  142 143
```

$$n_1 = 2$$

```
 0  1    8  9   16 17  | 72  73   80  81   88  89
 2  3   10 11   18 19    74  75   82  83   90  91
 4  5   12 13   20 21    76  77   84  85   92  93
 6  7   14 15   22 23    78  79   86  87   94  95
24 25   32 33   40 41    96  97  104 105  112 113
26 27   34 35   42 43 +  98  99  106 107  114 115
28 29   36 37   44 45   100 101  108 109  116 117
30 31   38 39   46 47   102 103  110 111  118 119
48 49   56 57   64 65   120 121  128 129  136 137
50 51   58 59   66 67   122 123  130 131  138 139
52 53   60 61   68 69   124 125  132 133  140 141
54 55   62 63   70 71 | 126 127  134 135  142 143
```

$$n_1 = 4$$

```
 0  1    6  7   12 13  | 72  73   78  79   84  85
 2  3    8  9   14 15    74  75   80  81   86  87
 4  5   10 11   16 17    76  77   82  83   88  89
18 19   24 25   30 31    90  91   96  97  102 103
20 21   26 27   32 33    92  93   98  99  104 105
22 23   28 29   34 35 +  94  95  100 101  106 107
36 37   42 43   48 49   108 109  114 115  120 121
38 39   44 45   50 51   110 111  116 117  122 123
40 41   46 47   52 53   112 113  118 119  124 125
54 55   60 61   66 67   126 127  132 133  138 139
56 57   62 63   68 69   128 129  134 135  140 141
58 59   64 65   70 71 | 130 131  136 137  142 143
```

$$n_1 = 3$$

```
 0  1   12 13   24 25  | 72  73   84  85   96  97
 2  3   14 15   26 27    74  75   86  87   98  99
 4  5   16 17   28 29    76  77   88  89  100 101
 6  7   18 19   30 31    78  79   90  91  102 103
 8  9   20 21   32 33    80  81   92  93  104 105
10 11   22 23   34 35    82  83   94  95  106 107
36 37   48 49   60 61 + 108 109  120 121  132 133
38 39   50 51   62 63   110 111  122 123  134 135
40 41   52 53   64 65   112 113  124 125  136 137
42 43   54 55   66 67   114 115  126 127  138 139
44 45   56 57   68 69   116 117  128 129  140 141
46 47   58 59   70 71 | 118 119  130 131  142 143
```

$$n_1 = 6$$

E.2.3 $f_1 = 3, f = 6$

```
 0  1  2    6  7  8  | 72  73  74    78  79  80
 3  4  5    9 10 11    75  76  77    81  82  83

12 13 14   18 19 20    84  85  86    90  91  92
15 16 17   21 22 23    87  88  89    93  94  95

24 25 26   30 31 32    96  97  98   102 103 104
27 28 29   33 34 35    99 100 101   105 106 107

36 37 38   42 43 44   108 109 110   114 115 116
39 40 41   45 46 47   111 112 113   117 118 119

48 49 50   54 55 56   120 121 122   126 127 128
51 52 53   57 58 59   123 124 125   129 130 131

60 61 62   66 67 68   132 133 134   138 139 140
63 64 65   69 70 71  | 135 136 137   141 142 143
```
$n_1 = 2$

```
 0  1  2   12 13 14  | 72  73  74    84  85  86
 3  4  5   15 16 17    75  76  77    87  88  89
 6  7  8   18 19 20    78  79  80    90  91  92
 9 10 11   21 22 23    81  82  83    93  94  95

24 25 26   36 37 38    96  97  98   108 109 110
27 28 29   39 40 41    99 100 101   111 112 113
30 31 32   42 43 44   102 103 104   114 115 116
33 34 35   45 46 47   105 106 107   117 118 119

48 49 50   60 61 62   120 121 122   132 133 134
51 52 53   63 64 65   123 124 125   135 136 137
54 55 56   66 67 68   126 127 128   138 139 140
57 58 59   69 70 71  | 129 130 131   141 142 143
```
$n_1 = 4$

```
 0  1  2    9 10 11  | 72  73  74    81  82  83
 3  4  5   12 13 14    75  76  77    84  85  86
 6  7  8   15 16 17    78  79  80    87  88  89

18 19 20   27 28 29    90  91  92    99 100 101
21 22 23   30 31 32    93  94  95   102 103 104
24 25 26   33 34 35    96  97  98   105 106 107

36 37 38   45 46 47   108 109 110   117 118 119
39 40 41   48 49 50   111 112 113   120 121 122
42 43 44   51 52 53   114 115 116   123 124 125

54 55 56   63 64 65   126 127 128   135 136 137
57 58 59   66 67 68   129 130 131   138 139 140
60 61 62   69 70 71  | 132 133 134   141 142 143
```
$n_1 = 3$

```
 0  1  2   18 19 20  | 72  73  74    90  91  92
 3  4  5   21 22 23    75  76  77    93  94  95
 6  7  8   24 25 26    78  79  80    96  97  98
 9 10 11   27 28 29    81  82  83    99 100 101
12 13 14   30 31 32    84  85  86   102 103 104
15 16 17   33 34 35    87  88  89   105 106 107

36 37 38   54 55 56   108 109 110   126 127 128
39 40 41   57 58 59   111 112 113   129 130 131
42 43 44   60 61 62   114 115 116   132 133 134
45 46 47   63 64 65   117 118 119   135 136 137
48 49 50   66 67 68   120 121 122   138 139 140
51 52 53   69 70 71  | 123 124 125   141 142 143
```
$n_1 = 6$

E.2.4 $f_1 = 2, f = 12$

0 1	4 5	8 9	12 13	16 17	20 21
2 3	6 7	10 11	14 15	18 19	22 23
24 25	28 29	32 33	36 37	40 41	44 45
26 27	30 31	34 35	38 39	42 43	46 47
48 49	52 53	56 57	60 61	64 65	68 69
50 51	54 55	58 59	62 63	66 67	70 71
72 73	76 77	80 81	84 85	88 89	92 93
74 75	78 79	82 83	86 87	90 91	94 95
96 97	100 101	104 105	108 109	112 113	116 117
98 99	102 103	106 107	110 111	114 115	118 119
120 121	124 125	128 129	132 133	136 137	140 141
122 123	126 127	130 131	134 135	138 139	142 143

$n_1 = 2$

0 1	8 9	16 17	24 25	32 33	40 41
2 3	10 11	18 19	26 27	34 35	42 43
4 5	12 13	20 21	28 29	36 37	44 45
6 7	14 15	22 23	30 31	38 39	46 47
48 49	56 57	64 65	72 73	80 81	88 89
50 51	58 59	66 67	74 75	82 83	90 91
52 53	60 61	68 69	76 77	84 85	92 93
54 55	62 63	70 71	78 79	86 87	94 95
96 97	104 105	112 113	120 121	128 129	136 137
98 99	106 107	114 115	122 123	130 131	138 139
100 101	108 109	116 117	124 125	132 133	140 141
102 103	110 111	118 119	126 127	134 135	142 143

$n_1 = 4$

0 1	6 7	12 13	18 19	24 25	30 31
2 3	8 9	14 15	20 21	26 27	32 33
4 5	10 11	16 17	22 23	28 29	34 35
36 37	42 43	48 49	54 55	60 61	66 67
38 39	44 45	50 51	56 57	62 63	68 69
40 41	46 47	52 53	58 59	64 65	70 71
72 73	78 79	84 85	90 91	96 97	102 103
74 75	80 81	86 87	92 93	98 99	104 105
76 77	82 83	88 89	94 95	100 101	106 107
108 109	114 115	120 121	126 127	132 133	138 139
110 111	116 117	122 123	128 129	134 135	140 141
112 113	118 119	124 125	130 131	136 137	142 143

$n_1 = 3$

0 1	12 13	24 25	36 37	48 49	60 61
2 3	14 15	26 27	38 39	50 51	62 63
4 5	16 17	28 29	40 41	52 53	64 65
6 7	18 19	30 31	42 43	54 55	66 67
8 9	20 21	32 33	44 45	56 57	68 69
10 11	22 23	34 35	46 47	58 59	70 71
72 73	84 85	96 97	108 109	120 121	132 133
74 75	86 87	98 99	110 111	122 123	134 135
76 77	88 89	100 101	112 113	124 125	136 137
78 79	90 91	102 103	114 115	126 127	138 139
80 81	92 93	104 105	116 117	128 129	140 141
82 83	94 95	106 107	118 119	130 131	142 143

$n_1 = 6$

E.2.5 $f_1 = 4,\ f = 12$

0	1	2	3	8	9	10	11	16	17	18	19
4	5	6	7	12	13	14	15	20	21	22	23
24	25	26	27	32	33	34	35	40	41	42	43
28	29	30	31	36	37	38	39	44	45	46	47
48	49	50	51	56	57	58	59	64	65	66	67
52	53	54	55	60	61	62	63	68	69	70	71
72	73	74	75	80	81	82	83	88	89	90	91
76	77	78	79	84	85	86	87	92	93	94	95
96	97	98	99	104	105	106	107	112	113	114	115
100	101	102	103	108	109	110	111	116	117	118	119
120	121	122	123	128	129	130	131	136	137	138	139
124	125	126	127	132	133	134	135	140	141	142	143

$$n_1 = 2$$

0	1	2	3	16	17	18	19	32	33	34	35
4	5	6	7	20	21	22	23	36	37	38	39
8	9	10	11	24	25	26	27	40	41	42	43
12	13	14	15	28	29	30	31	44	45	46	47
48	49	50	51	64	65	66	67	80	81	82	83
52	53	54	55	68	69	70	71	84	85	86	87
56	57	58	59	72	73	74	75	88	89	90	91
60	61	62	63	76	77	78	79	92	93	94	95
96	97	98	99	112	113	114	115	128	129	130	131
100	101	102	103	116	117	118	119	132	133	134	135
104	105	106	107	120	121	122	123	136	137	138	139
108	109	110	111	124	125	126	127	140	141	142	143

$$n_1 = 4$$

0	1	2	3	12	13	14	15	24	25	26	27
4	5	6	7	16	17	18	19	28	29	30	31
8	9	10	11	20	21	22	23	32	33	34	35
36	37	38	39	48	49	50	51	60	61	62	63
40	41	42	43	52	53	54	55	64	65	66	67
44	45	46	47	56	57	58	59	68	69	70	71
72	73	74	75	84	85	86	87	96	97	98	99
76	77	78	79	88	89	90	91	100	101	102	103
80	81	82	83	92	93	94	95	104	105	106	107
108	109	110	111	120	121	122	123	132	133	134	135
112	113	114	115	124	125	126	127	136	137	138	139
116	117	118	119	128	129	130	131	140	141	142	143

$$n_1 = 3$$

0	1	2	3	24	25	26	27	48	49	50	51
4	5	6	7	28	29	30	31	52	53	54	55
8	9	10	11	32	33	34	35	56	57	58	59
12	13	14	15	36	37	38	39	60	61	62	63
16	17	18	19	40	41	42	43	64	65	66	67
20	21	22	23	44	45	46	47	68	69	70	71
72	73	74	75	96	97	98	99	120	121	122	123
76	77	78	79	100	101	102	103	124	125	126	127
80	81	82	83	104	105	106	107	128	129	130	131
84	85	86	87	108	109	110	111	132	133	134	135
88	89	90	91	112	113	114	115	136	137	138	139
92	93	94	95	116	117	118	119	140	141	142	143

$$n_1 = 6$$

E.2.6 $f_1 = 3$, $f = 12$

```
  0   1   2     6   7   8  | 12  13  14    18  19  20
  3   4   5     9  10  11    15  16  17    21  22  23

 24  25  26    30  31  32    36  37  38    42  43  44
 27  28  29    33  34  35    39  40  41    45  46  47

 48  49  50    54  55  56    60  61  62    66  67  68
 51  52  53    57  58  59  + 63  64  65    69  70  71

 72  73  74    78  79  80    84  85  86    90  91  92
 75  76  77    81  82  83    87  88  89    93  94  95

 96  97  98   102 103 104   108 109 110   114 115 116
 99 100 101   105 106 107   111 112 113   117 118 119

120 121 122   126 127 128   132 133 134   138 139 140
123 124 125   129 130 131 | 135 136 137   141 142 143

                     n₁ = 2
```

```
  0   1   2    12  13  14 | 24  25  26    36  37  38
  3   4   5    15  16  17   27  28  29    39  40  41
  6   7   8    18  19  20   30  31  32    42  43  44
  9  10  11    21  22  23   33  34  35    45  46  47

 48  49  50    60  61  62    72  73  74    84  85  86
 51  52  53    63  64  65  + 75  76  77    87  88  89
 54  55  56    66  67  68    78  79  80    90  91  92
 57  58  59    69  70  71    81  82  83    93  94  95

 96  97  98   108 109 110   120 121 122   132 133 134
 99 100 101   111 112 113   123 124 125   135 136 137
102 103 104   114 115 116   126 127 128   138 139 140
105 106 107   117 118 119 | 129 130 131   141 142 143

                     n₁ = 4
```

```
  0   1   2     9  10  11 | 18  19  20    27  28  29
  3   4   5    12  13  14   21  22  23    30  31  32
  6   7   8    15  16  17   24  25  26    33  34  35

 36  37  38    45  46  47    54  55  56    63  64  65
 39  40  41    48  49  50    57  58  59    66  67  68
 42  43  44    51  52  53  + 60  61  62    69  70  71

 72  73  74    81  82  83    90  91  92    99 100 101
 75  76  77    84  85  86    93  94  95   102 103 104
 78  79  80    87  88  89    96  97  98   105 106 107

108 109 110   117 118 119   126 127 128   135 136 137
111 112 113   120 121 122   129 130 131   138 139 140
114 115 116   123 124 125 | 132 133 134   141 142 143

                     n₁ = 3
```

```
  0   1   2    18  19  20 | 36  37  38    54  55  56
  3   4   5    21  22  23   39  40  41    57  58  59
  6   7   8    24  25  26   42  43  44    60  61  62
  9  10  11    27  28  29   45  46  47    63  64  65
 12  13  14    30  31  32   48  49  50    66  67  68
 15  16  17    33  34  35   51  52  53    69  70  71

 72  73  74    90  91  92    108 109 110   126 127 128
 75  76  77    93  94  95    111 112 113   129 130 131
 78  79  80    96  97  98    114 115 116   132 133 134
 81  82  83    99 100 101    117 118 119   135 136 137
 84  85  86   102 103 104    120 121 122   138 139 140
 87  88  89   105 106 107 |  123 124 125   141 142 143

                     n₁ = 6
```

E.2.7 $f_1 = 6$, $f = 12$

```
 0   1   2   3   4   5  | 12  13  14  15  16  17
 6   7   8   9  10  11    18  19  20  21  22  23

24  25  26  27  28  29    36  37  38  39  40  41
30  31  32  33  34  35    42  43  44  45  46  47

48  49  50  51  52  53    60  61  62  63  64  65
54  55  56  57  58  59    66  67  68  69  70  71

72  73  74  75  76  77    84  85  86  87  88  89
78  79  80  81  82  83    90  91  92  93  94  95

96  97  98  99 100 101   108 109 110 111 112 113
102 103 104 105 106 107  114 115 116 117 118 119

120 121 122 123 124 125  132 133 134 135 136 137
126 127 128 129 130 131  138 139 140 141 142 143
```
$$n_1 = 2$$

```
 0   1   2   3   4   5  | 24  25  26  27  28  29
 6   7   8   9  10  11    30  31  32  33  34  35
12  13  14  15  16  17    36  37  38  39  40  41
18  19  20  21  22  23    42  43  44  45  46  47

48  49  50  51  52  53    72  73  74  75  76  77
54  55  56  57  58  59    78  79  80  81  82  83
60  61  62  63  64  65    84  85  86  87  88  89
66  67  68  69  70  71    90  91  92  93  94  95

96  97  98  99 100 101   120 121 122 123 124 125
102 103 104 105 106 107  126 127 128 129 130 131
108 109 110 111 112 113  132 133 134 135 136 137
114 115 116 117 118 119  138 139 140 141 142 143
```
$$n_1 = 4$$

```
 0   1   2   3   4   5  | 18  19  20  21  22  23
 6   7   8   9  10  11    24  25  26  27  28  29
12  13  14  15  16  17    30  31  32  33  34  35

36  37  38  39  40  41    54  55  56  57  58  59
42  43  44  45  46  47    60  61  62  63  64  65
48  49  50  51  52  53    66  67  68  69  70  71

72  73  74  75  76  77    90  91  92  93  94  95
78  79  80  81  82  83    96  97  98  99 100 101
84  85  86  87  88  89   102 103 104 105 106 107

108 109 110 111 112 113  126 127 128 129 130 131
114 115 116 117 118 119  132 133 134 135 136 137
120 121 122 123 124 125  138 139 140 141 142 143
```
$$n_1 = 3$$

```
 0   1   2   3   4   5  | 36  37  38  39  40  41
 6   7   8   9  10  11    42  43  44  45  46  47
12  13  14  15  16  17    48  49  50  51  52  53
18  19  20  21  22  23    54  55  56  57  58  59
24  25  26  27  28  29    60  61  62  63  64  65
30  31  32  33  34  35    66  67  68  69  70  71

72  73  74  75  76  77   108 109 110 111 112 113
78  79  80  81  82  83   114 115 116 117 118 119
84  85  86  87  88  89   120 121 122 123 124 125
90  91  92  93  94  95   126 127 128 129 130 131
96  97  98  99 100 101   132 133 134 135 136 137
102 103 104 105 106 107  138 139 140 141 142 143
```
$$n_1 = 6$$

E.3 Two progressive factors

E.3.1 $f_1 = 2$, $f_2 = 4$, $f = 12$

```
  0   1     4   5    16  17 | 20  21    32  33    36  37
  2   3     6   7    18  19   22  23    34  35    38  39

  8   9    12  13    24  25   28  29    40  41    44  45
 10  11    14  15    26  27   30  31    42  43    46  47

 48  49    52  53    64  65   68  69    80  81    84  85
 50  51    54  55    66  67 _ 70  71    82  83    86  87
                            +
 56  57    60  61    72  73   76  77    88  89    92  93
 58  59    62  63    74  75   78  79    90  91    94  95

 96  97   100 101   112 113  116 117   128 129   132 133
 98  99   102 103   114 115  118 119   130 131   134 135

104 105   108 109   120 121  124 125   136 137   140 141
106 107   110 111   122 123 |126 127   138 139   142 143
```

$$n_1 = 2, \quad n_2 = 4$$

```
  0   1     4   5    24  25 | 28  29    48  49    52  53
  2   3     6   7    26  27   30  31    50  51    54  55

  8   9    12  13    32  33   36  37    56  57    60  61
 10  11    14  15    34  35   38  39    58  59    62  63

 16  17    20  21    40  41   44  45    64  65    68  69
 18  19    22  23    42  43   46  47    66  67    70  71
 _                          +                           _
 72  73    76  77    96  97  100 101   120 121   124 125
 74  75    78  79    98  99  102 103   122 123   126 127

 80  81    84  85   104 105  108 109   128 129   132 133
 82  83    86  87   106 107  110 111   130 131   134 135

 88  89    92  93   112 113  116 117   136 137   140 141
 90  91    94  95   114 115 |118 119   138 139   142 143
```

$$n_1 = 2, \quad n_2 = 6$$

```
  0   1     6   7    24  25 | 30  31    48  49    54  55
  2   3     8   9    26  27   32  33    50  51    56  57
  4   5    10  11    28  29   34  35    52  53    58  59

 12  13    18  19    36  37   42  43    60  61    66  67
 14  15    20  21    38  39   44  45    62  63    68  69
 16  17    22  23    40  41   46  47    64  65    70  71
 _                          +                           _
 72  73    78  79    96  97  102 103   120 121   126 127
 74  75    80  81    98  99  104 105   122 123   128 129
 76  77    82  83   100 101  106 107   124 125   130 131

 84  85    90  91   108 109  114 115   132 133   138 139
 86  87    92  93   110 111  116 117   134 135   140 141
 88  89    94  95   112 113 |118 119   136 137   142 143
```

$$n_1 = 3, \quad n_2 = 6$$

E.3.2 $f_1 = 2,\ f_2 = 6,\ f = 12$

```
 0  1    4  5    8  9  | 24 25   28 29   32 33        0  1    4  5    8  9  | 36 37   40 41   44 45
 2  3    6  7   10 11    26 27   30 31   34 35         2  3    6  7   10 11    38 39   42 43   46 47
12 13   16 17   20 21    36 37   40 41   44 45        12 13   16 17   20 21    48 49   52 53   56 57
14 15   18 19   22 23    38 39   42 43   46 47        14 15   18 19   22 23    50 51   54 55   58 59

48 49   52 53   56 57    72 73   76 77   80 81        24 25   28 29   32 33    60 61   64 65   68 69
50 51   54 55   58 59    74 75   78 79   82 83        26 27   30 31   34 35    62 63   66 67   70 71
60 61   64 65   68 69    84 85   88 89   92 93
62 63   66 67   70 71    86 87   90 91   94 95        72 73   76 77   80 81    108 109  112 113  116 117
                                                      74 75   78 79   82 83    110 111  114 115  118 119
96 97   100 101  104 105   120 121  124 125  128 129  84 85   88 89   92 93    120 121  124 125  128 129
98 99   102 103  106 107   122 123  126 127  130 131  86 87   90 91   94 95    122 123  126 127  130 131
108 109 112 113  116 117   132 133  136 137  140 141  96 97   100 101  104 105   132 133  136 137  140 141
110 111 114 115  118 119 | 134 135  138 139  142 143  98 99   102 103  106 107 | 134 135  138 139  142 143

          n₁ = 2, n₂ = 4                                          n₁ = 2, n₂ = 6
```

$n_1 = 2,\ n_2 = 4$

$n_1 = 2,\ n_2 = 6$

```
 0  1    6  7   12 13  | 36 37   42 43   48 49
 2  3    8  9   14 15    38 39   44 45   50 51
 4  5   10 11   16 17    40 41   46 47   52 53

18 19   24 25   30 31    54 55   60 61   66 67
20 21   26 27   32 33    56 57   62 63   68 69
22 23   28 29   34 35    58 59   64 65   70 71

72 73   78 79   84 85    108 109  114 115  120 121
74 75   80 81   86 87    110 111  116 117  122 123
76 77   82 83   88 89    112 113  118 119  124 125

90 91   96 97   102 103   126 127  132 133  138 139
92 93   98 99   104 105   128 129  134 135  140 141
94 95   100 101  106 107 | 130 131  136 137  142 143

               n₁ = 3, n₂ = 6
```

$n_1 = 3,\ n_2 = 6$

E.3.3 $f_1 = 3$, $f_2 = 6$, $f = 12$

```
 0   1   2    6   7   8  | 24  25  26   30  31  32
 3   4   5    9  10  11    27  28  29   33  34  35
12  13  14   18  19  20    36  37  38   42  43  44
15  16  17   21  22  23    39  40  41   45  46  47

48  49  50   54  55  56    72  73  74   78  79  80
51  52  53   57  58  59  _ 75  76  77   81  82  83
60  61  62   66  67  68 + 84  85  86   90  91  92‾
63  64  65   69  70  71    87  88  89   93  94  95

96  97  98  102 103 104   120 121 122  126 127 128
99 100 101  105 106 107   123 124 125  129 130 131
108 109 110 114 115 116   132 133 134  138 139 140
111 112 113 117 118 119 | 135 136 137  141 142 143
```

$$n_1 = 2, n_2 = 4$$

```
 0   1   2    6   7   8  | 36  37  38   42  43  44
 3   4   5    9  10  11    39  40  41   45  46  47
12  13  14   18  19  20    48  49  50   54  55  56
15  16  17   21  22  23    51  52  53   57  58  59
24  25  26   30  31  32    60  61  62   66  67  68
27  28  29   33  34  35    63  64  65   69  70  71

72  73  74   78  79  80    108 109 110  114 115 116
75  76  77   81  82  83    111 112 113  117 118 119
84  85  86   90  91  92    120 121 122  126 127 128
87  88  89   93  94  95    123 124 125  129 130 131
96  97  98  102 103 104    132 133 134  138 139 140
99 100 101  105 106 107 | 135 136 137  141 142 143
```

$$n_1 = 2, n_2 = 6$$

```
 0   1   2    9  10  11  | 36  37  38   45  46  47
 3   4   5   12  13  14    39  40  41   48  49  50
 6   7   8   15  16  17    42  43  44   51  52  53
18  19  20   27  28  29    54  55  56   63  64  65
21  22  23   30  31  32    57  58  59   66  67  68
24  25  26   33  34  35    60  61  62   69  70  71

72  73  74   81  82  83    108 109 110  117 118 119
75  76  77   84  85  86    111 112 113  120 121 122
78  79  80   87  88  89    114 115 116  123 124 125
90  91  92   99 100 101    126 127 128  135 136 137
93  94  95  102 103 104    129 130 131  138 139 140
96  97  98  105 106 107 | 132 133 134  141 142 143
```

$$n_1 = 3, n_2 = 6$$

References

Andrews, W. S. (1917) *Magic squares and cubes*, 2nd edn. Chicago: Open Court Publishing Company [Republished unaltered (with chapters by other writers) by Dover Publications, New York (1960).]

Ball, W. W. R. (1908) *A short account of the history of mathematics*, 4th edn. London: Macmillan.

Ball, W. W. R. (1939) *Mathematical recreations and essays*, 11th edn (ed. H. S. M. Coxeter). London: Macmillan.

Bellew, J. (1997) Counting the number of compound and Nasik magic squares. *Mathematics Today* (*Bulletin of the Institute of Mathematics and its applications*) **33** (4), 111–118.

Besslich, Ph. W. (1983) Comments on electronic techniques for pictorial image reproduction. *IEEE Transactions on Communications* **31**, 846–847.

Brouwer, A. E. (1991) Recursive constructions of mutually orthogonal Latin squares. In *Latin squares: new developments in the theory and applications* (ed. J. Dénes and A. D. Keedwell), pp. 149–168. Amsterdam: North-Holland.

Brown, J. W., Cherry, F., Most, L., Most, M., Parker, E. T. and Wallis, W. D. (1993) Completion of the spectrum of orthogonal diagonal Latin squares. In *Graphs, matrices, and applied mathematics* (ed. R. S. Rees), *Lecture notes in pure and applied mathematics* **139**, 43–49.

Dénes, J. and Keedwell, A. D. (1974) *Latin squares and their applications*. London: Academic Press.

Euler, L. (1779) Recherches sur une nouvelle espèce de quarrés magiques. Memoir presented to the Academy of Sciences of St Petersburg on 8 March 1779. [Republished in *Leonhardi Euleri Opera Omnia* (1) **7**, 291–392 (1923).]

Frénicle de Bessey, B. (1693) Des quarrez ou tables magiques. In *Divers ouvrages de mathématique et de physique par messieurs de l'Académie Royale des Sciences* (ed. P. de la Hire, Sedileau and Pothenot), pp. 423–507. Paris: l'Imprimerie Royale.

Frost, A. H. (1866) Invention of magic cubes, and construction of magic squares possessing additional properties. *Quarterly Journal of Mathematics* **7**, 92–101.

Frost, A. H. (1878) On the general properties of Nasik squares. *Quarterly Journal of Mathematics* **15**, 34–49.

Gardner, M. (1996) The magic of 3 × 3. *Quantum* **6** (3), 24–26.

Gould, H. W. (1972) *Combinatorial identities; a standard set of tables listing 500 binomial coefficient summations*, revd edn. Morgantown, West Virginia: West Virginia University.

Graham, R. L., Knuth, D. E. and Patashnik, O. (1989) *Concrete mathematics*, 2nd edn. Menlo Park, California: Addison-Wesley.

Hardy, G. H. (1940) *A mathematician's apology*. Cambridge University Press.

Hollingdale, S. (1989) *Makers of mathematics*. Harmondsworth: Penguin Books.

Kraitchik, M. (1930) *La mathématique des jeux ou récréations mathématiques*. Brussels: Stevens Frères.

McClintock, E. (1897) On the most perfect forms of magic squares, with methods for their production. *American Journal of Mathematics* **19**, 99–120.

Ollerenshaw, K. (1986) On 'most perfect' or 'complete' 8 × 8 pandiagonal magic squares. *Proceedings of the Royal Society of London* A**407**, 259–281.

Ollerenshaw, K. (1989) Living mathematics: introduction to the 25th anniversary issue. *Bulletin of the Institute of Mathematics and its Applications* **25**, 50–56.

Ollerenshaw, K. and Bondi, H. (1982) Magic squares of order four. *Philosophical Transactions of the Royal Society of London* A**306**, 443–532.

Petkovšek, M., Wilf, H. S. and Zeilberger, D. (1996) *A = B*. Wellesley, Massachusetts: Peters.

Planck, C. (1919) Pandiagonal magic squares of orders 6 and 10 with minimal numbers. *The Monist* **29**, 307–316.

Riordan, J. (1956) *An introduction to combinatorial analysis*. London: Chapman & Hall.

Rosser, B. and Walker, R. J. (1939) The algebraic theory of diabolic magic squares. *Duke Mathematical Journal* **5**, 705–728.

Sallows, L. (1997) The lost theorem. *The Mathematical Intelligencer* **10**, 51–54.

Xu, C.-X. and Lu, Z.-W. (1995) Pandiagonal magic squares. In *Computing and combinatorics* (Proceedings of the first annual international computing and combinatorics conference, COCOON 95) (ed. D.-Z. Du and M. Li), *Lecture notes in computer science* **959**, 388–391.

Index

Entries marked with an asterisk are defined in the Glossary.

A

Andrews, W.S., 3, 147
arrays*, 2, 3, 5, 12, 20–22, 24, 25, 35, 37, 38, 40, 55, 94, 96, 97, 106, 108–113, 124
auxiliary square*, 4–11, 14, 15, 86, 87, 95, 97, 114–123
   mixed*, 8, 9, 15, 86, 97, 115, 119–123
   orthogonal*, 4, 7, 8, 116, 119
   radix*, 4, 14, 15, 85, 86, 97, 114–117, 119
   unit*, 4, 15, 85, 86, 97, 114–117, 119

B

Ball, W. W. Rouse, ii, 3, 7, 147
Bellew, James, 8, 9, 15, 86, 87, 115, 119–121, 147
Besslich, Dr. Ph. W., xiii, 12, 147
binomial* coefficients, xiv, 17, 59, 64–70, 75, 84, 90, 93, 99, 100, 102–104
Black, David, 2
block*, 16, 17, 19, 38–55, 62–64, 67, 89–95, 97, 125
   building* procedure, 48, 50, 54, 93, 95
   corner*, 16, 17, 39–43, 46–51, 53–55, 62–64, 67, 91–95, 97, 134
   largest corner*, 16, 17, 39, 41, 48–54, 62–64, 67, 73–75, 92, 93, 95, 125, 134, 135
   smallest corner*, 41–47, 49, 51, 85, 86, 92, 94, 134
Bondi, Sir Hermann, ix, xiv, 127, 148
Brée, David S., 89, 90, 121
Bremen University, xiii, 12
broken diagonal *see* diagonal
Brouwer, A. E., 1, 147
Brown, J. W., 4, 5, 147

C

Chaundy, Theodore, xiii
combinatorics*, x, 94

complementary*, 23, 25–30, 37, 92, 94, 107, 109, 111–113, 133
complements*, 4, 12, 20, 22, 23, 25, 26, 94, 96, 107, 128–131
configuration, 52, 53
configurations of largest corner block, $F_n(f)$, 16, 50, 54, 62, 63, 73, 75
   enumeration, 53, 54, 93
construction of principal reversible squares *see* principal reversible squares
construction of successively larger blocks *see* successively larger blocks
correspondence, one-to-one*, 16, 19, 33, 36, 38, 87, 95, 130, 132
couplet*, 12, 23, 94, 97, 106, 107, 128–131
cross sums, equal, 10, 23, 25, 35, 37–39, 45, 47, 48, 94, 96, 97, 106, 108–113, 123, 124

D

Dénes, J., 1, 147
diagonal
   broken*, 2, 4, 8, 20, 21, 25, 94, 95, 98, 115
   principal*, 2–6, 8, 20, 25–27, 29, 94, 96, 97, 108–110, 115, 124
diagonal Latin square *see* Latin square
Doherty, Paul, xv
Dürer, Albrecht, 4

E

enumeration of principal reversible squares *see* principal reversible squares
enumeration of progressive factors *see* progressive factors
enumeration of progressive paths *see* progressive paths
enumeration of reversible squares in a set *see* reversible squares in a set
equal* cross sums *see* cross sums, equal
essentially different squares*, 2, 9, 13, 16, 19, 26–28, 30, 71, 83, 88, 93, 96, 97, 117, 118, 124, 127

Euler, Leonhard, ii, xiii, 1, 4, 6, 8, 15, 115, 119, 147

F
factor table*, 55–59, 62, 91–94, 96
Flude, Ronald, xiv
Franklin, Benjamin, 4
Frénicle de Bessey, Bernard, 4, 147
Frost, the Revd Andrew H., 6, 7, 12, 15, 86, 115, 116, 118, 119, 147, 148
Frost, the Revd Percival, 6

G
gap* > 1, 42, 43, 45–47, 49, 53, 54, 85, 91, 94
Gardner, Martin, 3, 89, 148
Goatly, Dr M. B., xv
Gould, H. W., 72, 148
Graham, Ronald L., xiv, 100, 148

H
Hardy, G. H., xiii, 148
Hollingdale, Stuart, 100, 104, 148
hyper algorithm, 72

I
I.M.A., x, xv, 13
image processing , xiii, 1
inverse transformation*, 34, 36–38, 98, 114

K
Keedwell, A. D., 1, 147
King's School, Canterbury, xv
knight's path*, 8–10, 15, 86, 87, 95, 115, 119–123
Knuth, Donald E., xiv, 100, 148
Kraitchik, M., 3, 4, 6, 148

L
Ladybarn House School, Manchester, xiv
Lancaster University, xiv
Latin square*, 1, 4–6, 10, 86, 94, 115
    diagonal*, 5, 95, 147
    orthogonal*, 5, 6, 10, 95, 115, 147
    self-orthogonal*, 95
layer* of blocks, 48, 51, 63, 95, 134
layering* process *see* block, building procedure
legitimate transformations of reversible squares*, 16, 19, 25–30, 39, 71, 83, 88, 98, 105, 109, 114
lo-shu, 3
Lu, Zhun-Wei, 6, 10, 148

M
McClintock, Eamon, 2, 12–14, 87, 89, 90, 115, 128–131, 148

McClintock square*, 12–15, 87, 89, 97, 115, 128–132
magic square*, ix, xiii, xiv, 1–12, 16, 17, 19–21, 71, 87, 90, 97, 115–119, 121–123, 125–128, 147, 148
Manchester University, xv
mixed auxiliary square *see* auxiliary square
most-perfect square*, ix, xiii–xv, 2, 12–17, 19–22, 29–33, 35–39, 51, 72, 73, 83, 85–89, 92, 93, 97, 98, 105, 114, 115, 128–133, 148

N
Nasik square*, 6, 147
Newton, Sir Isaac, ii, 99, 104
Newton's backward triangle, 100
non-intersecting paths *see* paths
normal square*, 2, 7, 97, 98
normalized primitive square* *see* primitive square

O
Ollerenshaw, Dame Kathleen, xiii, xiv, 2, 4, 13, 14, 70, 85, 87, 88, 121, 127, 131, 148
    I.M.A. Christmas Lecture, 13
one-to-one correspondence *see* correspondence, one-to-one
orthogonal auxiliary square *see* auxiliary square
orthogonal Latin square *see* Latin square

P
Painter, Richard, xv
pandiagonal magic square*, xiii, 1–3, 6–12, 14, 16, 17, 20–22, 38, 72, 73, 85, 87, 90, 97, 115–119, 121–123, 125–128, 148
    singly-even, 7, 8, 73
Parkinson, Robert, xv
Pascal, Blaise, 99, 104
Pascal triangle, 90, 99–102, 104
Patashnik, Oren, xiv, 100, 148
path*, 6–11, 15, 19, 55, 56, 58, 86, 87, 91–93, 95, 96, 98, 115–123
    permissible*, 121
paths, non-intersecting*, 9, 10, 95, 116–118, 121
perforated sheets, 51
Petkovšek, M. 72, 84, 148
Planck, C., 7, 8, 148
Pollock, Paul, xv
primitive square*, 10, 11, 15, 25, 33, 35, 36, 38, 48, 85, 87, 90, 97, 115, 123–128, 132
    normalized, 10, 11, 15, 48, 90, 97, 123, 124, 126–128, 132
principal diagonal *see* diagonal
principal reversible* square, 13, 16, 17, 28–31,

35, 39–42, 45–47, 49–53, 62–64, 70, 71, 73, 83–88, 91–94, 96, 131–135
principal reversible squares
    construction, 16, 19, 28, 29, 39–41, 45, 49–52, 72, 73, 87, 128–134
    enumeration, N_n, 19, 29, 63, 70, 71, 73, 83, 84, 87–90, 93, 135
progressive factors*, 17, 48, 49, 52–56, 58, 62, 73–77, 80, 83, 88, 92, 93, 96, 120, 125–128, 134, 135
    enumeration, $W_y(n)$, 55, 59, 63, 64, 74, 75, 79, 84, 93, 126–128
progressive path*, 55–59
progressive paths, enumeration, 55–58, 74

R
radix auxiliary square *see* auxiliary square
reflection*, 2, 4, 12, 26, 27, 29, 35, 96, 97, 108–110, 117, 131
reverse similarity*, 16, 23, 24, 29, 37–39, 42, 44, 46, 47, 51, 52, 96, 108–113
reversible square*, ix, 15–17, 19, 20, 22–42, 44, 45, 47–53, 62–64, 70–73, 83–94, 96–98, 105, 108–114, 120, 125, 131–133
    4 by 4, 28, 35, 51
    8 by 8, 85
    top row of, 28, 34, 42, 46, 49–50, 53, 54, 85, 86, 96, 97, 114, 120, 124, 126–130, 132
reversible squares in a set, enumeration, M_n, 13, 19, 27, 28, 30, 63, 70, 71, 85, 93
Riordan, John, 80, 148
Rosser, Barkley, 10–12, 15, 25, 33, 48, 85, 87, 90, 111, 112, 115, 123, 126, 127, 148

S
S-complements*, 20, 22, 23, 25, 96, 107, 128–131
St Andrew's cross, 8
St Leonards School, St Andrews, xiv
Sallows, Lee, 3, 148
self-orthogonal square*, 6
set* of reversible squares, 16, 19, 27–31, 39, 71, 85, 93, 96, 114, 123, 126, 127, 131, 132

similar*, 12, 16, 23, 29, 39, 40, 96, 97, 128
    blocks, 16, 17, 39–41, 43–49, 53, 54, 91, 92, 95, 97
    rows and columns, 16, 25, 40, 47, 97, 128
Simon, Herbert A., xv
singly-even pandiagonal magic square *see* pandiagonal magic square
Somerville College, Oxford, xiv
Stanford University, xv
step*, 7, 8, 58, 98, 120, 121, 130
successively larger blocks, construction, 47–50, 73

T
Tarry, 4
transformation*
    most-perfect square into reversible square, 16, 36–38, 98, 114
    reversible square into most-perfect square, 2, 13, 16, 33–36, 51, 98, 114, 133
Trinity College, Cambridge, xiii
triple identity (I.12), 90, 102, 103

U
unit auxiliary square *see* auxiliary square
universe, age of, 2

V
Vandermonde, Alexandra, 102

W
Walker, R. J., 10–12, 15, 25, 33, 48, 85, 87, 90, 111, 112, 115, 123, 126, 127, 148
Wilf, H. S., 148

X
Xu, Cheng-Xu, 6, 10, 148

Y
Yii, Emperor of China, 3

Z
Zeilberger, D., 72, 84, 148

Do-it-yourself kit for constructing largest corner blocks

An analogy for the result of the method of construction of largest corner blocks is that of overlying **transparent perforated sheets**, as it were of sheets of postage stamps of different size with the stamps representing blocks. The widths and depths of the stamps on successive sheets must both be integral (> 1) multiples, respectively, of those on sheets lying below, corresponding to any selection of the progressive factors of n given by the equations (4.4.4.1) and (4.4.4.2).

If the sheets were to be hinged together with those of larger stamps being placed in alignment above those of smaller stamps, with top-left corners overlying each other, then a pin pushed through any perforation of any of the sheets would always penetrate through to the bottom sheet containing the smallest stamps. If the diagrams on the following pages (where small circles represent perforations) are photocopied on to transparencies, and the corners correctly aligned, then the logic of the structure of largest corner blocks is clearly apparent.

0	1	4	5	24	25	28	29	96	97	100	101	120	121	124	125
2	3	6	7	26	27	30	31	98	99	102	103	122	123	126	127
8	9	12	13	32	33	36	37	104	105	108	109	128	129	132	133
10	11	14	15	34	35	38	39	106	107	110	111	130	131	134	135
16	17	20	21	40	41	44	45	112	113	116	117	136	137	140	141
18	19	22	23	42	43	46	47	114	115	118	119	138	139	142	143
48	49	52	53	72	73	76	77	144	145	148	149	168	169	172	173
50	51	54	55	74	75	78	79	146	147	150	151	170	171	174	175
56	57	60	61	80	81	84	85	152	153	156	157	176	177	180	181
58	59	62	63	82	83	86	87	154	155	158	159	178	179	182	183
64	65	68	69	88	89	92	93	160	161	164	165	184	185	188	189
66	67	70	71	90	91	94	95	162	163	166	167	186	187	190	191
192	193	196	197	216	217	220	221	288	289	292	293	312	313	316	317
194	195	198	199	218	219	222	223	290	291	294	295	314	315	318	319
200	201	204	205	224	225	228	229	296	297	300	301	320	321	324	325
202	203	206	207	226	227	230	231	298	299	302	303	322	323	326	327
208	209	212	213	232	233	236	237	304	305	308	309	328	329	332	333
210	211	214	215	234	235	238	239	306	307	310	311	330	331	334	335
240	241	244	245	264	265	268	269	336	337	340	341	360	361	364	365
242	243	246	247	266	267	270	271	338	339	342	343	362	363	366	367
248	249	252	253	272	273	276	277	344	345	348	349	368	369	372	373
250	251	254	255	274	275	278	279	346	347	350	351	370	371	374	375
256	257	260	261	280	281	284	285	352	353	356	357	376	377	380	381
258	259	262	263	282	283	286	287	354	355	358	359	378	379	382	383